GDAŃSK
THE CITY OF MY DREAMS
SOPOT – GDYNIA

Tessa

Gdańsk, The City of My Dreams

Photo authors:	**Stanisław Składanowski, Bogumiła Piazza**
	and: **Zbigniew Kosycarz** (p. 10), **Janusz Rydzewski** (p. 13), **Maciej Kostun** (p. 114)
Text authors:	**Krzysztof Berenthal,** Stanisław Sikora, Edward Klamann
Postcards:	**Krzysztofa Berenthala**
Photo editor:	**Bogumiła Piazza**
Computer layout:	**STUDIO JUSTA Gdańsk**

© **TESSA. tel. +48 600 075 458, fax (+48 58) 552 20 97; e-mail: tessa@wydawnictwo.com.pl**

ISBN 83-88882-45-7

GDAŃSK
A THOUSAND YEAR HISTORY

Towns are established for a variety of reasons. It could be the ruler's whim or defense considerations, but commercial reasons are the commonest. Commodity exchange has, since the origin of mankind, determined the importance of the locations used for this purpose. Gdańsk was such a place. Apart from the military and political purposes, it was trade and economics that resulted in the city's origin, its ups and downs. The crossroads of trade routes and freedom of commodity exchange, the influx of business-oriented merchants from Germany and other countries of Europe as well as the enormous commodity resources and receptive market of the Polish and Lithuanian lands were the foundation of the city's power. From a provincial capital it turned quite rapidly into a European city, very different from the other cities of the Republic of Poland. To somewhat simplify matters, the millennial history of Gdańsk can be divided into five periods. Each one represents a distinct image of the city, bearing on the following period. The first period is the early Middle Ages with the city establishing its position as a local capital and seaport. Then came the "Teutonic" period and the formation of a powerful commercial centre within the Hanseatic League. After the Thirteen-years' war, the city extraordinarily flourished, gaining many privileges and a huge economic base in the former Poland and its satellite countries.

Gdańsk in fact became an economic key to the Republic of Poland. The next period brought the invasion of Gdańsk by Prussia, its fall and rise from crisis, the ravages of the Napoleonic wars, the Free City and destruction in 1945. It is now difficult to state whether the last, post-war period was favourable for the city. This will largely depend on our succes-

sors and us. The history of Gdańsk was mostly written by German and Polish historians. Both had an ambition-driven and patriotic ("nationalistic") attitude to the subject matter. The city's history was considered a banner that one must plant in one's land.

Nonetheless Gdańsk had its own life, its political views and a great sense of independence. It was above all guided by its own economic benefit. The city's social structure, its political ambitions and economic potential could be likened to Italian city-states or rather, as the Gdańsk patricianship thought, to the city-republics of antiquity. This was favoured by the specific political and legal detachment from Royal Prussia, resulting from the different mode and time of union with the Republic of Poland. The Prussian middle class managed more secure position than the rest of the Republic of Poland, owing to its support in the Thirteen-Years' War. More than 60% of the townspeople were immigrants from Germany or their descendants. The prevalent language was German, yet hardly any city in the Republic of Poland could boast so many speeches that are today interpreted as anti-German. The expansion of the Teutonic Knights Order to Gdańsk Pomerania and other Polish lands had been perceived by Poles (since the 10-11th c.) as a manifestation of the German "drang nach Osten". When Teutonic Knights, in 1308, took Gdańsk, where apart from the Polish borough and Osiek there had already been a colony of German merchants, this occupation of Gdańsk was nothing else but the infamous Gdańsk massacre.

Out of the three settlements existing then, the Teutonic Knights trusted the least the above mentioned settlement of German merchants, which was awarded municipal rights as late as in 1343 (as the Right or Main City - Recht Stadt). They willingly endorsed the Polish settlement right (Old Town) to the former borough with a majority of Slavonic people. The Thirteen-years war was instigated by a riot of German-origin middle class and Polish-origin noblemen, who were the Teutonic Order's subjects. It was nothing but the money of the German middle class that had led to the failure of the Order. It is impossible to see any nationalist or political intentions in their behaviour. The middle class of Gdańsk and other towns of the Teutonic State simply considered it profitable to unite with the great commodity market of the Republic of Poland and to embrace the freedoms it could offer. Throughout most of its history Gdańsk was the scene of sharp economic divisions and although it witnessed numerous social and religious upheavals, extremely rarely did it demonstrate its political views. We can infer from this that the inhabitants of Gdańsk believed in the principle that politics compromises trade. If we assumed that they did not know much about politics, the thesis would be defendable. It was hardly political, though very generous, of the town to have supported King Stanisław Leszczyński, in fact defeated, and to have borne all the consequences of this act.

The fierce resistance of the town to Frederick the Great can be assessed likewise. In both cases Gdańsk made, in a way, a typically "Polish" mistake. The anticipated ally was far away while the opponent and danger were at the gates. There was, however, some logic to this policy. Fidelity to the Republic of Poland, so willingly evoked by Poles and so carefully erased by Germans. A fidelity demonstrated with some exaggeration, as no other city in the Republic of Poland had so many Polish eagles within its walls! A fidelity that resulted from capitalist calculation. Gdańsk owed its power to the Vistula basin and was fully aware of that. As a result of the second partition of Poland, Gdańsk forfeited the link with its natural economic resources, the Republic of

Poland. Its European-level trade started to decline and the whole economic system of the city with it. Wealthy families emigrated or shared the city's lot. Immigrants, including Jews, flowed in from Prussia and they partly took over the city's commerce and crafts. After almost half a century of stagnation, Gdańsk entered a new era in its history - and became a provincial industrial port.

For a city that for almost 500 years had ranked amongst the most eminent in Europe, this was a downfall with far-reaching consequences. The city's community had been exchanged and transformed. The influx of people with a different mentality assigned the city a new role and a new geographic position. Communication routes, decorative buildings and customs had changed. It was at that time that the Gdańsk in, and over which, the second world war broke out began to emerge, beyond people's awareness. A war that turned the city into rubble, so that today there are only crumbs left. These crumbs are the cultural heritage or what has survived of it. We are now endeavouring to recreate these long forgotten remnants of tradition to overcome the feelings of emptiness, dissatisfaction and demotivation. Only if we comprehend this portion of the surviving cultural heritage and the consequences of its conservation, are we entitled to speak of its continuation as its heirs and successors.

Krzysztof Berenthal

AN OUTLINE OF HISTORY OF GDAŃSK

The name Gdańsk was first recorded in 999 by the biographer of St. Adalbert (św. Wojciech), the Benedictine monk Jan Kanapariusz, as Gyddanyzc, which stems from the old Slavic name of Gdaniesk. Both of these names are derived from the prefix gd- which indicates "wetness" or "dampness". The settlement which was the beginning of today's city was on the marshy terrain along the passageway across the former arm of the Vistula (Wisła) River, which is currently known as the Motława River. The name of this river undoubtedly comes from the now-extinct Prussian language (1283 - Mutulava). The alteration in the name could have occurred in the thirteenth century when large numbers of Prussians settled in Gdańsk seeking the protection of Prince Świętopełek from the Teutonic Knights. The German name Danzig, however, is the transformation and vulgarization of the original word Gdańsk (1148 - Kdanzc, 1263 - Danzk, 1311 - Danczk, 1399 - Danczik, 1645 - Dantzigk).

The oldest traces of inhabitance were found in the Oliwa area and date from 2500-1700 BC. During the Roman era (early first century AD to 375), the area was visited by traders from the south in search of so-called "Baltic gold" or amber, and later, from the seventh to the ninth centuries, Arab traders even found their way here. It was in the ninth century that Gdańsk was established as an agricultural, craft and fishing settlement of about 300 inhabitants in the area of the Long Market (Długi Targ). In approximately 975, possibly on the initiative of Prince Mieszko I who ruled the Vistula Coastal (Pomorze Nadwiślańskie) area, as is documented in the Dagome iudex act of 991, a stronghold with a fishing and craft settlement was established just to the north of the initial settlement. It was from this stronghold that, for nearly two centuries, the rulers maintained control over the port adjacent to it, and, thus, the river traffic on the Vistula (Wisła) River. In 997, St Adalbert

(św. Wojciech) Sławnikowic took it upon himself to go and, as Kanapariusz writes, "… fight the Prussian gods and statues, as the land was in close vicinity and was known from the memoirs of Prince" (Bolesław Chrobry). Thus acquainted with his wishes, the prince gave Adalbert a boat and 30 armed men to assure him a safe journey. Adalbert arrived first in Gdańsk (primo urbem Gyddanyzc), which lay on the border of the prince's vast holdings on the sea coast. Here, by the mercy of God who had provided for his safe passage, Adalbert christened a large crowd of people. This probably took place on Easter Saturday 27 March 997.

Subisław was a descendent of the area's governors mentioned earlier, and was the first in the dynasty of east-Pomeranian princes based in Gdańsk who fought with Pomeranians, Danes, Prussians, Brandenburgers and Teutonic Knights in defense of the city. The greatest of these princes was Świętopełk I, also known later as the Great (ca. 1220-1266), who, in definitively severing ties with the sovereignty of the Piast princes, made significant contributions to the development of Gdańsk. In approximately 1227, he granted Gdańsk a city charter under Lübeck law, and brought the Dominican order from Kraków in order to strengthen the still weak hold Christianity had on his land. Under the rule of his son, Mściwoj I (1266-1294), whose political position was significantly weaker than that of his father's, a strong city government in Gdańsk was created and its deputies (consules) are first mentioned in the historical record in 1274. In 1296, as stipulated by the Kępno treaty of 1284, following the death of Mściwoj (1294) the eastern Pomeranian principality came under the rule of Prince Przemysł of Greater Poland (Wielkopolska), later Przemysław II, King of Poland. The Gdańsk

Pomorze area was involved in the insidious occupation of arming the Teutonic Knights in 1308-1309, thus contributing to the ouster of the lawful ruler, Prince Łokietek of the Brzesko-kujawska area. It was under his reign that the seal of the city bearing the inscription Sigillum burgensium in Dantzike was first used in 1299. During Teutonic times, the multi-partite character of the city's urban plan was consolidated, and three distinct and independent bodies existed side by side. These were the Main Town (Główne Miasto - also known as the Right Town (Prawe Miasto) from "the town on the right") including the Old Suburb (Stare Przedmieścia), the Old Town (Stare Miasto) and the New Town (Młode

shipbuilding centre and its largest city with a population of approximately 20,000 citizens in 1460. Gdańsk maintained numerous contacts with the most important economic and financial centres throughout Europe.

At the beginning of the sixteenth century, Gdańsk, with a population of about 36-37 thousand inhabitants, quickly accepted the new religious ideas that were sweeping across western Europe, namely Lutheranism and Calvinism, and Catholicism became the minority faith. Under the influences of the Reformation and western Europe, patrician culture and art were shaped and the city took on a democratic atmosphere. The Gothic style gave way to the Renaissance and northern Euro-

*Old Packing House (**Stara Pakownia**) on the bank of the Nowa Motława (early twentieth century). The picturesque port was full of ships, barges and rafts.*

Miasto). The most economically powerful of the three, the Main Town, had approximately 10,000 inhabitants, and after receiving limited Lübeck law in 1342, surrounded itself with moats and defensive walls and began its most important building projects - the city hall and St. Mary's Church. In 1361, city representatives first took part in a meeting of the League of Hanseatic Cities; Gdańsk would play an important role in the organisation for the next several centuries. After Teutonic rule had been overthrown, the Gdańsk region accepted Polish sovereignty and was incorporated into Poland in 1454, thus obtaining advantageous privileges from King Kazimierz Jagiellończyk which permitted unprecedented development and the legal ownership of approximately 1,000 km2 of outlying terrain. This was in return for the significant political, military and especially financial support the city gave to Poland during the so-called Thirteen Year War with the Teutonic Order (1454-1466). Over the course of barely a century, the city was transformed from one whose principal activity was trading grain and forestry products into Poland's main port, its

pean Mannerism became popular under the influence of the Netherlands. In the second half of the century, the population of Gdańsk reached approximately 50,000 and included immigrants from Franconia, Rhineland, Brandenburg and other German lands; there were also new citizens from Holland, England, Scotland, France and Italy. The tolerant religious climate of the city coupled with the patronage of the city and its patricians meant that thousands of superb artists (ca. 3,150 masters - in Kraków there were 714 at this time) and craftsmen (ca. 20,000) found employment in the city, especially during the so-called golden age from 1580 to 1650. Thanks to their efforts some of the most exquisite works in Poland and Europe were created. Simultaneously, many architectural projects were carried out including municipal buildings, over 300 granaries, beautiful residences and monumental fortifications whose rings of ramparts, bastions and moats surrounded the entire city. Residential developments were begun in the lower terrain that lay to the east of the historic city, which became known as the Lower City (Dolne Miasto). By the mid-seventeenth century Gdańsk had become the largest metropolis in the Baltic Sea basin with a population of almost 77,000. The city's allegiance to Poland was expressed by its citizens when the Commonwealth was under the greatest threat. During the first Polish-Swedish war (1625-1629), the city was especially loyal when it did not allow the attackers to penetrate its wall and in thanks received special commendations from the Parliament on three occasions, in 1626, 1628, and 1629. One of them was for the Battle of Oliwa in which the Gdańsk navy defeated the Swedish flotilla near Jelitkowo in the Gulf of Gdańsk on 28 November 1627.

During the second war with Sweden (1655-1660), Gdańsk (along with Zamość and Jasna Góra in Częstochowa) again refused to surrender to the aggressors. The anniversary of the Polish-Swedish peace treaty, signed on 3 May 1660, was designated as an annual holiday and was even celebrated after Poland had been partitioned. Another dramatic event took place when the city defended King Stanisław Leszczyński, who was hiding within its walls, as Russian and Saxon armies laid siege to it from early February to early July 1734. During this time, several hundred citizens were killed, approximately 1,800 residences were destroyed and over 100 granaries were burned.

Despite the severity of these events, Gdańsk's worst days were yet to come. During the first partition of Poland, the city lost its

Długi Targ had undoubtedly been a marketplace until the 1920s and the presence of the nearby port could be sensed here.

outlying terrain, Hel and Szkarpawa. Joanna Schopenhauer wrote of the Prussian King Frederick II "…he is a vampire which sucks the life blood from the city…" as he forced the city into almost total economic collapse by the imposition of embargoes. Although the city made persistent diplomatic attempts to avoid falling under Prussian rule, the expense was so high that the inevitable occurred in 1793. The new rulers revoked nearly all the privileges that had been bestowed upon the city by the Polish kings. Economic stagnation and other problems slowly began to drive the city's citizens away, and its population fell to barely 36,000. Hope among the remaining residents of Gdańsk was rekindled in late May 1807 when, after a two-month siege, the French army marched into the city. The status of free city was given to Gdańsk under the Treaty of Tylża that was signed by Emperor Napoleon Bonaparte. After the emperor's defeat at Moscow and a siege that lasted nearly eight months, the Napoleonic Army, including Polish legionnaires, left Gdańsk in early January 1813. Under the agreements of the Vienna Congress of 1815, Gdańsk was returned to the Prussians. There was a certain degree of economic recovery in the second half of the nineteenth century especially after the opening of the railway lines between Gdańsk and Tczew in 1852 and Gdańsk and Szczecin in 1870. Industry slowly began to grow; the turnover in the commercial port, which was moved from the Motława River to New Port (Nowy Port), increased, shipbuilding began to develop at the Klawitter Shipyard, and other branches of industry, principally armaments, began to expand. At the close of the nineteenth century, large-scale works were undertaken to dismantle the fortifications to the north and west of the city. This allowed for the re-development of the transportation system and enlarged the area available for residential building. Despite strong Germanization, the Polish identity survived in Gdańsk and many Polish religious, cultural and educational and other organisations were founded.

Gdańsk had about 175,000 residents in 1914, 15% of them Poles, but population growth was much slower here than in other cities in the country of the Hohenzollerns. From the defeat of the Germans in 1918, a new hope was born among Poles that Gdańsk would return to the newly reborn

Commonwealth. The dilatory politics of the great powers, especially England, with regard to Germany destroyed these efforts. The Free City of Gdańsk was established under the Treaty of Versailles as a protectorate of the League of Nations to be represented by the High Commissioner. Approximately 356,000 residents (19% of them of Polish heritage) lived in this area of 1,893 km2 that stretched from Gdynia in the north almost to Tczew in the south. The complicated administrative structure of this "artificial creature" led to 70 legal and political confrontations between Poland and Gdańsk. Many of these were played out on the international stage, and as a result Polish-German relations were under constant strain, with Poland's western neighbor unable to accept the loss of Gdańsk. As soon as Hitler came to power in 1933, anti-Polish sentiment in Gdańsk began to grow with the spread of Fascism. The slogan " Return to the Reich" (zurück zum Reich) became the main propaganda theme of Gdańsk's German residents who directed their hatred mainly towards Polish railway workers, customs officers and postal employees. Despite the brutal fight against the Polish identity, it persevered thanks to the extraordinary efforts of the Gdańsk Polonia in the spheres of education, culture, science, religion, politics, propaganda and social and economic issues. September 1, 1939, the day on which the city's Fascist-controlled Senate illegally annexed the Free City to the Reich, was tragic for many Gdańsk citizens of Polish heritage who were either arrested and placed in concentration camps, expelled, or forced to emigrate. The Polish Post Office, whose 39 defenders were murdered, and Westerplatte, which was defended for almost seven days, became symbols of Polish bravery. When the war turned against the Germans and the front drew nearer to the coast, orders were received

from Hitler's Headquarters on 26 March 1945 to change Gdańsk into a fortress. After a bloody and vicious four-day fight, the Soviet Army took the city. The historic centre of the city had literally disappeared from the face of the earth, with 90% of it in ruins. Of 12,600 buildings, 60% were completely destroyed and more than 57,000 flats had ceased to exist; there was no electricity, gas or transportation. Many industrial operations were devastated as the liberating Soviet troops cleared out any of the machines, equipment and tools that had escaped destruction. The Soviets continued their criminal behaviour as they planned and systematically destroyed the surviving quarters.

Life in Gdańsk, however, was not fully extinguished; by 6 April 1945 the city had a president, followed by the first issue of the daily newspaper Dziennik Bałtycki on 19 May. A census taken on 16 June showed that 8,000 Poles and 124,000 Germans, most of whom had been forced to emigrate by 1946, were living in Gdańsk. The costly operation to clear up the 3 million m3 of rubble began almost immediately and a few years later rebuilding began which has continued uninterrupted until today.

The rebuilding of Gdańsk was not an issue that had been decided from the start. In writing the word "rebuilt", I am thinking more about today's urban form and historic atmosphere which can be found in reconstructed and stylized buildings.

The original concept of reconstructing Gdańsk's historical centre was to clear away the rubble, level the remaining buildings and to replace it with architecture in the spirit of social realism. The Main City was to have been partially planted with trees to create a kind of park

Gdańsk port canal in the 1920s was a very "crowded" place (even though it is much wider today).

Long Market (Długi Targ), 1945. The historic centre of Gdańsk (both the Main and Old Towns) were over 90% destroyed. Only one church and a few buildings had not been burned or shelled.

dotted with enclaves of preserved, historic architecture, such as St. Mary's Church (Kościół Mariacki), Artus Court (Dwór Artusa), and the Old Town Hall (Ratusz Staromiejski). Surrounding this, new housing estates were to have been built, like those in the Warsaw districts Praga II or MDM. The architecture in Wrzeszcz was also to have been significantly changed; for example, a housing estate like MDM was to have been built near the train station, a building of gigantic proportions, similar to Warsaw's Palace of Culture and Science (Pałac Kultury i Nauki) was to have been erected at the intersection of ul. Partyzantów and ul. Grunwaldzka. Fortunately, the planned demolition of the old buildings never occured, and only a small fragment of a promenade, today's ul. Klonowa, and some buildings were built. Political changes which occurred after 1954 allowed for the concept of Gdańsk's reconstruction to be changed and a new urban plan was developed, but this time, the city's cultural elite had much more influence on it. Waves of new residents continuously poured into Gdańsk in search of work, a roof over their heads or simply their niche in the world. Many of them came from the former Polish territories in the east, especially from the vicinity of Vilnius and, to a lesser extent, from Lviv. Among Gdańsk's growing population were a significant number of intellectuals including artists, scientists and art critics and historians. Many of them arrived with the love of their former eastern hometowns and bestowed it upon the new city just emerging from a sea of rubble. Throughout the disastrous postwar period, when first the

Soviet Red Army senselessly burned the city to the ground and several Polish authorities praised the destruction by saying "...finally the nest of Germanization and Drang nach Osten has been annihilated ...", Gdańsk also had some luck. The city was inhabited by intelligent people who grew to truly love it. It was they who were ultimately successful in convincing the state authorities that Gdańsk should be reconstructed to avoid criticism from the world that all traces of the German presence in the city had been eradicated. They saved the historical nucleus of the city. The first postwar guide to Gdańsk was written by Jan Kilarski, the author of the beautiful prewar Gdańsk monograph in the Polish Miracles (Cuda Polski) series. Reading this guidebook, one could wander the city streets and admire its beautiful monuments as if they were standing; in reality, the city lay in ruins.

Reconstruction began in the early 1950s in the Main City quarter between ul. Ogarna, ul. Garbary and ul. Długa. Several public buildings were erected - the post-office and the Leningrad cinema - and old buildings that had survived, including the city hall, the St. George shooting range (strzelnica św. Jerzego), and a majority of churches, were either secured or their reconstruction was begun. Work in earnest, however, did not begin until an urban plan, which outlined building priorities and introduced new transportation solutions, had been developed and approved in 1960.

Within ten years, the basic outline of the Main City had been rebuilt, and the majority the destruction in Wrzeszcz, Oliwa, Nowy Port and other city districts had been repaired.

The first building in the new Przymorze residential district, which was built using traditional brick construction, was completed in 1960. Soon after, preparations were made for the creation of the huge Przymorze housing estate, the so-called "bedroom of Gdańsk", which became a symbol of socialist house-building. Architects competed in creating ever larger buildings and this spurred the creation of the wave-shaped (falowiec) apartment blocks, thus named for their long, undulating facades. The first such buildings were small - only 350 m long - but later they reached lengths of up to 850 m. The empty spaces between Old Oliwa and the Baltic Sea shore were slowly filled in, and the area which had once served for Prussian army manoeuvers became a testing ground for architects and builders.

Combining the celebrations of Poland's millenium with the anniversary of ten centuries of Gdańsk secured new funds from the central budget for renovations and investments in the city, including the reconstruction of the Great Mill (Wielki Młyn), the Crane (Żuraw) and other buildings, and the renovation of the train station. The city's transportation system was also rebuilt, and new roads, like the so-called "Trasa W-Z" and Podwale Przedmiejskie, were created, and the Piastowski Junction was modernized along with Błędnik Bridge.

Universities and research institutions came to play an important role in the development of the city. By the end of the 1960s, Gdańsk had six institutions of higher education, five research institutions and 26 branches and departments of research and development institutions. The Gdańsk Technical University and the Medical Academy occupied the leading positions. At this time in Gdańsk, there was a total of 15,000 students, and it was this numerous and free-thinking group that initiated the violent protests of March 1968. The communist authorities effectively used propaganda to turn the workers against the students. The incidents of 1970 took a completely different turn, and although the core group of protesters was the shipyard workers, many students and some intellectuals joined in the clashes that lasted for three days. On Wednesday, 16 December, the situation changed dramatically after five shipyard workers were killed in front of the Gdańsk Shipyard gate; the strikes ended but tensions remained high. Relative peace was established when Edward Gierek, the new First Secretary of the Central Committee of the Polish Worker's Party (PZPR), visited in January 1971, and the government reversed their decision to increase food prices.

During the 1970's, there was a virtual storm of ideas in Gdańsk concerning modern architecture and urban development in the city centre. Fortunately, the majority of them were never realized, although some have still not died and continue to haunt like poltergeists. One of them is the 1960s - 1970s concept of the north-south route called the Red Road (Czerwona Droga) that disregards all existing historical and geographical realities. This spirit is still present among city planners and has a destructive impact on the development of the city.

*A detail of the Gdańsk Przymorze housing estate, erected in the early 1970s. The ten-story **wave-shaped (falowiec) apartment blocks** are characteristic this development. The block on ul. Obrońców Wybrzeża is approximately 850 m long and the other on ul. Jagiellońska is about 800 m long.*

11

The August strikes released unprecedented power, courage and hope in the citizens of Gdańsk. Outdoor masses held at Gate 2 drew thousands of people to both sides of the fence; access to the shipyard for non-employees was only by permission of the Inter-factory Strike Committee (MKS). The masses were not only an expression of spontaneous religious feeling, but were also a demonstration of the power of the rebellious public.

The closing of the civilian and military airport in Wrzeszcz and its move to the village of Rębiechowo, 10 km from the city, was not only a necessary move, but also a wise one. The terrain of the former airport became the site of the massive Zaspa housing estate. According to its planners, the new design of Zaspa was to have become a model for housing estates throughout Poland. In practice, another concrete bedroom was created.

The late 1970s were turbulent times in the Tri-City, and signals from Radom and Ursus fuelled an already hot atmosphere. Flowers were laid and meetings were held in front of Gdańsk Shipyard Gate 2 each December, and demonstrations on 11 November became a tradition. Therefore, the strike that broke out on 14 August 1980 was the rather logical consequence of earlier events. The atmosphere in the city at this time was akin to that during the Warsaw Uprising; everybody felt like pitching in and helping. Spontaneously, the shipyard was fully supplied with food, paper and other necessary items. A collection box for funds to build a Monument to the Fallen Shipyard Workers (Pomnik Poległych Stoczniowców) stood in front of the shipyard gates and every passer-by felt obliged to contribute. Negotiations between the newly formed trade unions (Międzyzakładowy Komitet Strajkowy), the only body representing the strikers, and the authorities were broadcast first on the shipyard's public address system and then on local radio. The day the agreements with the government delegation were signed was one of great happiness, despite the fact that many people doubted the lasting power of the documents. This feeling became increasingly strong as it appeared that the only

tangible achievement of the August strikes was the monument that was quickly rising in front of Gate 2. Although 13 December 1981 was a sunny day, martial law engulfed the city like a black cloud that darkened many people's lives for almost five years. The anguish of the first half of the 1980s was compensated for by the visit of Pope John Paul II to Gdańsk on 11 June 1987. The hope and happiness which the Pope instilled in the people of Gdańsk had to suffice for many years to come.

The most recent important event to take place in Gdańsk was the celebration of its millenium in 1997. The festivities lasted for almost a year and were as much applauded as maligned. A plan for the reconstruction and revitalisation of Granary Island was approved in 1998; it is the third such plan since 1947 for the island which is still covered by rubble. The only effective reconstruction in this area is the adaptation of the former electro-heating plant on Ołowianka Island as the new headquarters of the philharmonic orchestra.

*The euphoria of victory following the signing by the authorities of the so-called **August Agreements (Porozumienia Sierpniowe)** that ended the strike and, among other points, agreed to legalise the Solidarność Independent Trade Union (Niezależne Związki Zawodowe). At the time, it was the only institution in opposition to the communist authorities that was legal.*

*Discontinuing the dialogue with the people and the declaration of **martial law** were aimed at crushing the backbone of democratic opposition. Common acts of violence and the humiliation of ordinary citizens by intervention forces, especially by the militarized police (ZOMO), were symbolised by the police breaking into striking factories (Gate 2 at the Gdańsk Shipyard) and beating and killing strikers.*

The pilgrimage of John Paul II to Poland *in June 1987 revived the hope of the Polish people. His visit to Gdańsk was an important part of the pilgrimage, and the mass held in the Zaspa housing estate for nearly a million faithful from Gdańsk and other parts of Poland was a great experience. The fabulous, monumental altar in the shape of a galleon, designed by Marian Kołodziej and Lech Zaleski, carried its own special symbolism.*

The Renaissance **Upland Gate (Brama Wyżynna)** at ul. Wały Jagiellońskie is the beginning of the so-called Royal Route (Droga Królewska). Until the end of the nineteenth century, the gate was part of an enormous earthen and brick fortification wall to the west of which was a wide, deep moat. The gate, which guarded the main entrance to the city, was designed and built by Hans Kramer in 1574-1576. Its stone decorations, by Wilhelm van den Block in 1586-1588, included rustication and a frieze above the entablature with large crests of the Royal Prussians, Poland (with the Bull-calf or Ciołek crest of the Poniatowski family) and Gdańsk (the Hohenzollern crest was added on the eastern side in 1884). There are three Latin inscriptions beneath the crests; the middle one reads "Justice and piety are the foundations of all states". The Gothic buildings of the Przedbramie (literally - the area in front of the gate) on Long Street (ul. Długa) are visible in the background.

The **Przedbramie** (literally - the area in front of the gate) on Long Street (ul. Długa) is a medieval defensive complex that dates from the second half of the fourteenth century and was once an extension of the Long Street Gate (Brama Długouliczna) on the western side. It was expanded in the fifteenth and sixteenth centuries and transformed into a municipal prison at the end of the sixteenth century. Designed by Antoni van Obberghen and constructed by Jan Strakowski, it consists of the **Torture House (Katownia)**, with a reconstructed top, on the western side and the **Prison Tower (Wieża Więzienna)**, with its reconstructed cupola, that are connected by walls that form an internal courtyard. Part of the stone work from the destroyed St. James' Gate (Brama św. Jakuba) was used in the western wall of the Katownia, and decorative elements from destroyed townhouses were used in the northern wall on the courtyard side. The entrance which leads to the pillory's hanging bridge in the eastern wall of the Wieża Więzienna has been preserved. Today, part of the complex houses the Court and Law Museum of Gdańsk (Muzeum Sądownictwa i Prawa Gdańskiego) and the Museum of Amber is in the planning stages. The Golden Gate (Złota Brama) stands in the background.

A view of the foregate from the north, in the background – **St. George's Rifle Range**, the former seat of the elite shooting fellowship – a sort of a paramilitary organization. The rifle range also played the role of a social club. Constructed around 1494 and reconstructed after the war, it now serves as the seat of SARP (the Polish Architects Association).

The **Great Armoury (Wielka Zbrojownia)** is one of the most valuable examples of Dutch Mannerist architecture in Poland. From the Coal Market (Targ Węglowy) it resembles the houses of rich Gdańsk merchants more than it does an armoury, which it was until the nineteenth century. The **Straw Tower (Baszta Słomiana)** (fourteenth century), with its 4 m thick walls, was once used for gun powder storage and is adjacent to the **Great Armoury (Wielka Zbrojownia)** and in line with the Gothic defensive wall. Further to the north is the **Wybrzeże Theatre (Teatr Wybrzeże)** (not pictured) which was designed by Lech Kadłubowski and built in 1962-1966. Another interesting building is the **Old Pharmacy (Stara Apteka)** that dates from the first half of the seventeenth century.

Some of the sculptures were added to the facade at a later date. The Cossack figure is associated with a legend about the soldier's blind fidelity to a Wallachian Hospodar. The sculpture is an interesting relic as the square in front of the Armoury called Targ Węglowy (Coal Market), was the site for the execution of court punishments such as flogging, ridicule and - in special cases - capital punishment, until the 1700s.

The Millenium Tree (Drzewko Milenium), made of metal and decorated with symbolic gifts from Polish and foreign smiths, was erected on the Coal Market (Targ Węglowy) in 1997 to celebrate the Gdańsk Millenium. It was designed by Wojciech Schwartz and constructed by Leonard Dajkowski. The reconstructed high defensive wall covered by ivy is visible in the background. Only partially visible on the left is the **Straw Tower (Baszta Słomiana)** (fourteenth century) that is joined by a brick connector to the **Great Armoury (Wielka Zbrojownia)** (not pictured).

The building of Gothic defensive fortifications, including moats, walls, bastions, and towers, began in 1343 with the Corner Bastion *(Baszta Narożna)* (to the left) that surrounded the Main Town. The **Scouts' House (Dom Harcerza)** complex is adjacent to the **Corner Bastion (Baszta Narożna)** to the east; it is composed of seventeenth century buildings that were adapted after WWII. The fully reconstructed Gothic **Schultz Bastion (Baszta Schultza)**, named after J. C. Schultz, a nineteenth century engraver and enthusiast of Gdańsk's architectural monuments, and the partly reconstructed Gothic **Brewery Bastion (Baszta Browarna)** from the fourteenth century, are visible farther on.

The Rococo **Fahrenheit House (Dom Fahrenheita** - ul. Ogarna 94) dates from ca. 1760. It was rebuilt in 1953-1954 and the facade was reconstructed in 1960. Daniel Gabriel Fahrenheit (1686-1736), who was born and raised in this building, constructed a mercury thermometer using his own temperature scale in which water boils at 212°F. Parallel to Long Street (ul. Długa) and Long Market (Długi Targ), Ogarna Street (ul. Ogarna - properly Psia or Dog) is closed at its eastern end at the Motława River by the fifteenth century Cow Gate (Brama Krowia) that has been reconstructed from its foundations.

*(On previous page) The Renaissance **Golden Gate (Złota Brama)** on the right adjoins the Gothic Court of the **St. George Brotherhood (Dwór Bractwa św. Jerzego)** on the left. The gate, a wonderful example of the Italian style, was constructed by Jan Strakowski, according to a design by Abraham van den Block, in 1612-1614. Eight allegorical figures, made by Piotr Ringering in 1648 (reconstructed), adorn the attic of the gate on both sides and screen the roof. Among the Latin inscriptions on the gate, that from the side of ul.*

Długa reads "Small states grow in harmony - large states fall in discord". The palace is an example of Flemish building. It was built partially on the defensive walls (ground floor- arms storage, first floor - meeting, fencing and reception rooms) and was designed by Hans Glotau, in 1494, for the elite St. George Brotherhood. In the seventeenth century, the tent-like roof of the building was finished with a turret and a lamp (reconstructed) with a metal figure of St. George (copy, the original figure from 1556 is in the National Museum in Gdańsk).

(On next page) On previous page. A view through the Golden Gate of Długa Street, whose axis was intentionally bent to expose the town hall silhouette. This view has practically become a symbol of this part of town.

The Rococo-Classicist **Uphagen House (Dom Uphagena** - ul. Długa 12) wa erected in 1776 by Johann Beniamin Dreyer for the well-educated patrician Johan Uphagen, who, to protest the capture of Gdańsk by the Prussians, resigned h councillor's position in 1791. It was his will that the house become a museum and following postwar reconstruction and the partial restoration of its interic decor, it has become one. The large windows of the facade are accentuated by th clear vertical and horizontal divisions. The house's triangular peak is framed b volutes which sweep downward from the pediment across the two upper storie. The ground-floor portal is exceptional due to the crest of the house's owner an his wife, Abigail, which is located in the transom window.

The interiors of the rococo **Uphagen House** were meticulously recreated be tween 1980-99. Unfortunately most of the original fittings perished during th last war. The last owner wished the house to serve as a museum, to embellis and testify to the culture of Gdańsk. Most of the interiors and ornaments hav been painstakingly reconstructed, but will the soul of the Uphagens dwellin in details return?

The high-ceilinged entrance-hall in the **Uphagen House (Dom Uphagena)** is representative room which is characteristic for patrician homes in eighteent century Gdańsk. Invited guests and clients were greeted in the hall and then th party would move to other richly decorated rooms either on the ground or th first floor. In this house, for example, they would go to the red room - the livin room that was named after the colour of its damask wall-covering.

The ornaments on the tops and facades of the apart
ment houses in Gdańsk were a result of a certain de
gree of competition between the families living here
particularly in this "fashionable" street.

Houses Nos. 69 and 70 are amongst the few that surv
ved the war and retained their eclectic decor. The
facades date from 1896 and 1900, but their walls hid
older remains. - The motif of St. George was particu
larly popular in Gdańsk, the one from House No. 4
having been discovered recently.

Long Street (Ulica Długa - longa platea, 1331), com
monly known as the "salon of Gdańsk", is a continu
ation of the Royal Route. The street curves slightly from
the west, and the Main Town Hall (Ratusz Głównego
Miasta) closes it on the northern wall and the Koner
House (Dom Konerta) closes it on the southern side
At the far end of Long Market (Długi Targ), the exten
sion of Long Street (ul. Długa), is the Green Gate (Zie
lona Brama) which closes the square. This street wa
almost entirely destroyed in 1945 and the townhouse
that line it today are reconstructions that range from
fifteenth century Gothic to twentieth century pseudo
classicist. The townhouse at number 71 is specia
thanks to the preserved late-Gothic profiles from the
second half of the fifteenth century and the origina
Renaissance and Rococo elements that were added to
the peak of the building. Until the late nineteenth cen
tury there were porches on both sides of the street, bu
they were removed in order to improve traffic and to
make way for a street-car line (subsequently removed
in the 1960s).

This Renaissance townhouse was called the **Lion's Castle** (**Lwi Zamek** - ul. Długa 35) after the lion statues on the railings of the former porch. It was built by Hans Kramer in 1569 and was rich in sculptural decoration. A figure representing Fortune stands on the triangular peak, while the frieze in the reconstructed entrance-hall depicts Grammar, Arithmetic, Rhetoric and Geometry. It is here that the Schwartzwald family entertained King Władysław IV with a feast and dancing in 1636.

The southern frontage of Long Street (ul. Długa) is closed by a house dating from ca. 1560 known as the **Konert House** (**Dom Konerta**) after its first owner, or as the Schumann House (Dom Schumannów) after his heirs. It is regarded as one of the most beautiful patrician houses in Gdańsk. The classic motif of an entablature with a triglyph-metope frieze in which there are alternating rounded shields and bucrania is repeated on the three floors of the red facade. In defiance of the rule of superposition, these are supported only by Tuscan pilasters and garlands with figures of Greek gods (Zeus, Athena) at the top. Currently, the building is the headquarters of the Gdańsk Branch of the Polish Tourist Association (Oddział Gdańskiego Polskiego Towarzy-stwa Turystyczno-Krajoznawcze-go). A beautiful stone partition wall with three arcades above which there are bas-reliefs of Mercury, Juno and Neptune, and an entrance-hall, can currently be seen in the Old Town Hall (Ratusz Staromiejski).

The Gothic-Renaissance **Main Town Hall (Ratusz Głównego Miasta)**, the headquarters of the city council and its offices, was the most important municipal building in old Gdańsk. It was built by Henryk Ungeradin in 1379-1381 and then later expanded and modernised in the sixteenth century by Antoni van Oppberghen. Due to the preserved and reconstructed interiors such rooms as the Great Vestibule (Wielka Sień), the Great Hall of the Former Police-Administrative Court (Wielka Sala Wety), the Great Christopher Hall (Wielki Krzysztof), the Red Room (Sala Czerwona) - also known as the Great (Wielka) or Summer Council Hall (Letnia Sala Rady), the Winter (Zimowa) or Small Council Hall (Mała Sala Rady), the Small Hall of the Former Police-Administrative Court (Mała Sala Wety and Kamlaria), are all very interesting. Other rooms house both permanent and temporary exhibitions. This building was completely destroyed by fire and shell-marked in March 1945. After extensive reconstruction and renovation, it reopened on 1 April 1970 as the headquarters of the Gdańsk History Museum (Muzeum Historyczne Miasta Gdańska). Fragments of the frameworks of houses (ca. early fourteenth century) and defensive walls built by previous settlers have been discovered in the cellars.

The reconstructed Renaissance **dome** of the Main Town Hall (Ratusz Głównego Miasta) is 35 metres high, has three gloriettes and was made by the Gdańsk builder Dirk Daniels in 1561. The spire is topped by a large (2.03 m), gold-plated figure of King Zygmunt August (reconstructed), and four Jagiellonian eagles grace each of the corners. A reconstructed carillon hangs in the tower and replaces the one from 1560 by Johann Moor, the bell-founder from Brabandt. It is coupled with a clock that retains its original face. There is a beautiful view of the city and the surrounding areas from the top of the tower (48 m).

The atlantes supporting the cornice and landing of the Town Hall stairs. In between them there is an entrance to the cellar which used to be the depository for the goods of merchants who were under arrest. In between the atlantes passed the prisoners who were to wait in the basement for the Council's decision about their future.

The **Red Room (Czerwona Sala** - named after the colour of its damask wall-covering) i
the Main Town Hall (Ratusz Głównego Miasta), was jointly designed by Hans Vredeman d
Vries, the outstanding painter and theoretician of perspective, and the master wood-carve
Szymon Herle in 1589-1591. They divided the interior decoration into three zones: the firs
includes the floors, the benches near the walls, the portal and the fireplace; the second i
comprised of the lower molding and the frieze with its seven allegorical paintings; the thir
was made by Izaak van den Block, and includes the upper molding and the ceiling paint
ings framed in Herle's marvelous wood carvings. The famous painting "The Apotheosis o
Gdańsk" (Apoteoza Gdańska) from 1608 is here.

The magnificent **fireplace** made by sculptor Willem van der Meer (Bart the Younger) ir
1593 is in the Red Room (Czerwona Sala) of the Main Town Hall (Ratusz Głównego Miasta)
It is regarded as one of the most valuable Renaissance pieces in Gdańsk. Its base consist
of two muscular atlantes on either side of the fireplace that support the entablature with a
Doric frieze. Centered in the middle is a polychromed and gold-plated cartouche with the
crest of Gdańsk. The decoration of the fireplace is completed with inscriptions in Latir
warning the citizens of the consequences of betraying their own city.

The centre of the Red Room's ceiling is occupied by an oval painting entitled "An Apotheosis of the Liaison of Gdańsk with Poland" or "An Allegory of the Gdańsk Trade". Both names render the essence of the work although they express different ideas. In the centre of the painting there is a towering triumphal arch crowned with a very faithful city panorama from the early 1600s. The eagle on the town hall symbolises the protection (!) of the Republic of Poland and the hand of Providence is touching the tower of the Council's seat as if supporting it. It is also interesting to take a look at the perfectly represented city fortifications.

The portal connecting the town hall's vestibule, seen from the Red Room (the Council's summer room). Together with the cornice and the benches it is a marvelous example of woodcarving, a work of Szymon Herle. On the door one of the best preserved coats of arms of the City of Gdańsk.

Pre-war view of the Main City Hall vestibule is seemingly identical. However, the destruction of the plafond representing Fortune in a fire in 1945, of numerous decorative details and some flagstones from Delft was a serious loss.

The stairs in the Town Hall's vestibule are a reconstruction, and so are the balustrades in the mezzanine. The portal, beautifully carved in wood, and the door lead to the Council's summer room, called the Red Room. The portal is crowned with a magnificent Gdańsk coat of arms, on which the Polish Eagle built its nest, and the Sobieski coat of arms, "Janina" on its breast. It was beneath this that the councillors of Gdańsk used to pass when going to a session.

During the reconstruction of the Town Hall after the war, the appearance and decor of the White Room, or the Council Room, were completely transformed. Trials used to be held in here (until the 1700s). The present appearance is a quite contemporary concept alluding to the Renaissance. The stone portal leading to the room is authentic and it was transferred from the facade of one of the houses in Długa Street in the 19th c.

Artus Court (Dwór Artusa - *ul. Długi Targ 44),
originally the headquarters of the merchant
brotherhoods, later the stock exchange and a museum, is a Gothic construction dating from 1476-
1481 (the side on ul. Chlebnicka). The Manneris-
facade, designed by Abraham van den Block in
1616-1617 is interesting because it retains the
Gothic windows and rustication from 1552. Like-
nesses of King Zygmunt III Waza and his son
Władysław decorate the portal. The interior of
the monumental hall has a stellar-palm vaulted
ceiling supported by four richly decorated columns (fifteenth -nineteenth centuries). The eighteenth century late-Baroque Jurors' Old House
(Stary Dom Ławy) is to the left at number 45 and
to the right side at number 43 is the Baroque
Jurors' New House (Nowy Dom Ławy), also
known as the Vestibule of Gdańsk (Sień Gdańska)
because of its magnificent interior (seventeenth
and eighteenth centuries). At the beginning of the
twentieth century, it housed Lesser Giełdziński's
collections of applied art.*

The **tiled furnace** in Artus Court (Dwór Artusa) was made in 1545-1546 by George Stelzener, the construction worker Wolf and the painter Jost. Reaching a height of 11 metres, the furnace was the tallest in Europe at the time. It is made of several hundred colourful tiles, with eleven doubled images of rulers (including German Emperor Charles V), allegorical figures, ornamental motifs and the well-known set of Polish, Royal Prussian and Gdańsk crests. Its reconstruction, which was completed in 1995, is one of the greatest recent accomplishments of conservation work.

The former decor of Artus Court (view from the 1920s) was a result of accumulated layers, investments and alterations of decorations as well as of the changing use of the building over the centuries. Originally it was a symbol and element of the philosophy of the Hanza, a particular trade community. In time the court became a kind of a club for the bourgeois elites and a symbol of a particular democracy. Merchants' societies (guilds) occupied their designated seats (benches) here. Later on, other societies emerged. Each such fraternity had its patron saint. One of the biggest fraternities was St. Christopher's Bench. That is why there are so many images of the saint inside. It was also common to hang models of ships of Gdańsk merchants under the ceiling as the city was incredibly proud of its fleet.

The so-called **Gdańsk Vestibule** is an indispensable element of the interior in a Gdańsk house. This is where official meetings and balls were held, guests were received and business was conducted. The vestibule of the **Councillors House** played yet another role. King Zygmunt Waza III stayed here on several occasions. Thanks to Lesser Giełdziński, a merchant and outstanding collector from Gdańsk (19th c.), who exhibited his collections here, the vestibule was a kind of museum of Gdańsk art. The collections were lost during the last war and the vestibule's present appearance is a faithful reconstruction.

Lady in the Window is the title of a well-known novel by Deotyma, set in Gdańsk in the 17th c. Since both tourists and inhabitants had been in dispute about the location of the house and window from which the beautiful daughter of a wealthy inhabitant of Gdańsk was supposed to look out on the world, it was decided to resolve the problem once and for all. The ghost of "the lady in the window" was given suitable instructions and for some time she has been appearing regularly in the top window of the Council House, around noon, but also at other times on the hour.

ługi Targ is sometimes called the salon of Gdańsk. ↑ played the role of a marketplace from the 1200s ↑ probably even from the 900s. In the Renaissan- ↑ period, during a general rebuilding of the city, ↑ square was transformed to look like a Roman ↑rum. The principal portion of the square can be ↑en in the photo (north-western side). In the cor- ↑r are gathered the principal buildings of old ↑dańsk: the finely exposed Town Hall with a faca- ↑ rebuilt by Antoni van Obberghen in the 16th c. ↑ore to the right, the basically Gothic, but "cor- ↑cted" in the Renaissance style, facade of Artus ↑ourt, a building from the Hanza age evoking the ↑emocratic traditions of King Arthur and the Ro- ↑nd Table. Further to the right the Council House ↑ith the beautiful Gdańsk vestibule. The last buil- ↑ng in the photo is the **Golden House** - a renow- ↑ed burgher house.

↑he **Golden House (Złota Kamienica** - ul. Długa 41), with ↑s reconstructed upper part, is famous for the lavish gold- ↑lated bas-reliefs of historical and legendary scenes, fig- ↑res and ornamental decorations in the horizontal frieze ↑bove the entablature. Originally, the house was inhab- ↑ed by Mayor Hans Speymann (thus the name **Speyman ↑ouse (Dom Spey-mannów)**, and after 1786 it became ↑nown as the Steffens House (Dom Steffensów). It was de- ↑igned by Abraham van den Block and decorated by Johann ↑oigt of Rostoka in 1618-1618. Among the famous rulers ↑epicted in the plinths of the molding are two Polish kings ↑Władysław Jagiełło and Zygmunt Waza III. Its facade was ↑onstructed according to the classic superposition order, ↑ith Tuscan pilasters at the ground level, Ionic on the first ↑nd second floors, Corinthian on the third floor, and ↑annerist on the fourth floor.

The **Neptune Fountain**, standing at the focal point of the Long Market (Długi Targ), nowadays merely a fountain and a recognizable symbol, is one of akong several wells Długa Street and Długi Targ. All the wells in this representativ part of town were mostl decorated. This one, however, was the most important because of its location. It inspired a number of legends and tales. Its origin dates back to 1549. The present form of the fountain originated mostly in the 1600 and was modified (the bowl and body) in the 1700s.

The **Royal Houses (Kamienice Królewskie** - ul. Długi Targ 1-4). From the right: a classicist house dating from ca. 1800; a Renaissance house with a figure of Neptune (first half of the seventeenth century); two Baroque houses (second halves of the seventeenth and eighteenth centuries). Polish kings were entertained here, including Zygmunt Waza III (1623, 1626, 1627), Władysław IV (1635, 1636), Jan Kazimierz (1651, 1657, 1660), Jan Sobieski III (1677), August Sas II (1698) and Stanisław Leszczyński (1734). Prince Aleksander Sobieski was born on 9 September 1677 in the second house from the right.

The afore-mentioned "lady in the window" is not purely a literary fantasy. During her stay in Gdańsk around 1850, Deotyma (Jadwiga Łuszczewska, 1834-1908) lived with her mother in a lodging house located in the two apartment houses shown in the photo. During a visit to a Gdańsk mer-chant she came across a mysterious girl who se-emed to be hiding from people's eyes. The ro-mantic old interior of the house and the strange girl stirred the writer's ima-gination and a widely read novel was written as a result.

Old Gdańsk had several drawbridges, which proved that there was busy port life going on among the old buildings. Today, not a single bridge is raised to let a ship pass and the Green Bridge, above, has been waiting for councillors to decide on restoring its former function for years.

The buildings of former granaries, converted into offices, architecturally modernized and simplified, are merely a memory of what they were - the foundations of the city's former affluence.

Old Gdańsk port, stretched along the ban. of the Motława, once was full of charmir. ambiance and life, mostly concentrated of Granary Island, in places that today ne body would suspect of such activity. **St. gwie Mleczne** used to be the port's centr. A fragment of the Gothic **Stągiewna Ga (Brama Stągiewna)** is visible on Grana. Island (Wyspa Spichlerzy) which is su. rounded by the waters of the Old (Star. and New (Nowa) Motława rivers. The ga. consists of the lower **Stągiewka Bastio. (Baszta Stągiewka**, ca. 1456) and the up per **Stągwi Bastion (Baszta Stągwi**, 1515. Beyond a newly built quarter of stylize. townhouses (1997-1999) to the south of u. Stągiewna is **Stągiewny Bridge (Mo. Stągiewny)** which stands next to the gat. The panorama of the Main and Old tow. (Główne and Stare Miasto) up to the edg. of the Gdansk Heights (Wysoczyzn. Gdańska) opens up in the background.

(On next page) The **Long Quay (Długie Pobrzeże)** is a stone (formerly wooden) landing pier several hundred metres long on the left bank of the Motława River. Along it are reconstructed patrician houses, punctuated at intervals by defensive gates that close the streets perpendicular to the old port. These are the **Cow (Krowia)**, **Green (Zielona)**, **Chlebnicka**, **St. Mary (Mariacka)**, **Holy Ghost (Św. Ducha)**, **Crane (Żuraw)**, **St. John (Świętojańska)** and **Stall Keeper (Straganiarska) gates**, most of which date from the fifteenth century. Today it is a poplar promenade and Żegluga Gdańska SA operates a passenger ferry service near the, **Green Bridge (Zielony Most** - formerly Kogi)**. On the opposite side Granary Island (Wyspa Spichrzów) and a warehouse from the interwar period are partially visible. Ołowianka Island is further in the distance.

The Gothic **Chlebnicka Gate (Brama Chlebnicka** - ca. 1450) closes ul. Chlebnicka and on its Motława side is adorned with the oldest crest of Gdańsk - two crosses without a crown. A stylised lily decorates the other side of the gate, and its second name, Lily Gate, is derived from this. Further along is the reconstructed **Naturalists House** (Dom Przyrodników), with its characteristic alcove, and the adjacent **St. Mary Gate (Brama Mariacka)**.

Ruined for years, the wharves of Granary Island near the **Green Bridge** used to host famous Baltic and backwater sailing vessels that sailed from port to port and carried goods, but they also symbolised the dissapeared epoch of the Seamen.

The first house on the right is the late-Gothic **Schlieff House (Dom Schlieffów** - later **Lehmann House)** at ul. Chlebnicka 12 that dates from 1520, which can be seen from ul. Mariacka at the intersection of ul. Grząska. It is a full reconstruction as the original was dismantled in 1822 on the order of the Prussian King Frederick Wilhelm III and reconstructed on Peacock Island in Potsdam near Berlin, where it is known as Kavalierhaus. The fourth house in the row is the large **English House (Dom Angielski** - so-called as English merchants gathered here in the seventeenth century). It is also known as the **Angel House (Dom Pod Aniołami)** because of the decorative angel heads that adorn the facade. It was designed by Hans Kramer for Dirk Lillie in 1570. The outline of the roof of Chlebnicka Gate (Brama Clebnicka) is in the background.

The Renaissance **Association of Naturalists House (Dom Towarzystwa Przyrodniczego** - built in 1597) at Długie Pobrzeże, designed by Antoni van Obberghen for the merchant H. Koepe, was one of the tallest patrician houses of its time. It has been owned by the DTP since 1845, and has served as the headquarters of the Museum of Archeology (Muzeum Archeologii) since it was rebuilt after WWII. Primitive figures of early medieval pagan Prussian gods (baby), stand in front of the building. The chief architectural element of the building, the five story alcove and the slim tower with a lamp and a dome, is open to the public, to see the view from the top. On the right of this building is the St. Mary Gate (Brama Mariacka), a defensive Gothic construction from ca. 1485, which closes ul. Mariacka.

(On next page) Granary Island (Wyspa Spichrzów): on the left and right Długie Pobrzeże, bridges. This used to be the hub and the springboard for development of the former Gdańsk. Today it is just a pedestrian area.

The huge defensive gate closes Wide Street (ul. Szeroka), and the crane (Żuraw) wa the largest port crane in all of medieval Europe (built in 1442-1444). It is equippe with two pairs of wooden drums, 6 and 6.5 metres in diameter, which are put in motion by four workers treading on a staircase which allowed the crane, through complicated system, to lift a four-ton load to a height of 11 m and two-ton load to 2 m. It was reconstructed after WWII, and currently houses part of the Central Mar time Museum (Centralne Muzeum Morskie).

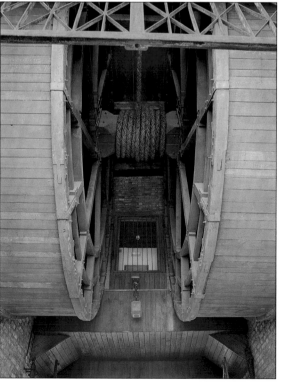

Ołowianka Island (Wyspa Ołowianka - the name originated from the storage here of non-ferrous metals) is surrounded by the waters of the Old Motława (Stara Motława) and th Stępce Canal (Kanał na Stępce - formerly Ciesielski). In the foreground are the three granaries that were reconstructed for the Central Maritime Museum (Centralne Muzeum Morskie the Olive (Oliwski - fifteenth century), Copper (Miedź - nineteenth century) and Maiden (Panna - seventeenth century). The old ore and coal carrier s/s Sołdek, the first ship built afte WWII in the Gdańsk Shipyard, in 1948, is moored here. Beyond this stands the Renaissance Royal Granary (Spichrz Królewski) built by Jan Strakowski in 1621, and in the backgroun the outline of the former Ołowianka heating factory from 1898 is visible. It was closed in 1997 and has been adapted into a modern concert hall for the Baltic Philharmonic.

The famed ore and coal carrier s/s Sołdek is moored at Ołowianka Island. It was launched in the Gdańsk Shipyard on 6 November 1948 and, as the first entirely Polish-built ship to b launched in the post-war period, it became the symbol of the Polish maritime industry. Today, it is a part of the Central Maritime Museum (Centralne Muzeum Morskie) in Gdańsk. Th ship was named after a shipyard foreman and tracer from the 1940s and his wife, Helena, was the vessel's godmother.

Just next to this is a piece of Gdańsk's most recent history. A **modern marina** was built in the New Motława (Nowa Motława) basin along the old wharf as part of the Gdańsk Millenium celebrations. It is the first such development within the city limits, and was designed to promote sailing and improve the city's image in the eyes of yachtsmen from western Europe. The area will be further developed to include hotels and other necessary facilities, such as baths, workshops, etc.

In the centre of the Main Town, the buildings destroyed during the war are "growing back". The **new apartment houses in Długie Pobrzeże** look out on the conversion of the old power station into a modern philharmonic hall.

The **Swan Tower** is a memory of the no longer existing Teutonic castle. The adjoining Fish Market was a place whose unique atmosphere attracted not only tourists, but artists as well.

(On previous page) On sunny days the city pa-norama is reflected in the water. Although th Fish Market (Targ Rybny) has not changed fc ages, it looks as though the other city, in th water's depths, contains something differer some ancient secret.

*Charming ul. **Mariacka** (whose proper name Panieńska after the Virgin Mary) is closed at i western end by the presbytery wall of the mon mental St. Mary's Church (Kościół Mariacki) ar in the east by the St. Mary Gate (Bram Mariacka). It was almost entirely destroyed the end of WWII. The original plan of fifteen century Gothic to nineteenth century Neo-Cla. sicist houses was faithfully reconstructed wit porches, cobbles and sewage canals runnin along the sides of the street. It is often visited t the people of Gdańsk and their visitors. Mar cafes and souvenir shops line the street to crea the unique atmosphere of this intriguing corne of the city.*

The fifteenth to
nineteenth century
p o r c h e s
(przedproża) that
lined ul. Mariacka
were reconstructed
from scratch with
much of the original
stonework, as were
the water outlets
named in Polish
rzygacze, plwacze
or gargulce, all of
which carry the
connotation of
spewing forth wa-
ter. For centuries
they were part of the
specific and unique
architecture of
Gdańsk and an ele-
ment of the patri-
cian lifestyle.

The **Gothic Church of the Most Holy Virgin Mary (Kościół Najświętsze[j] Marii Panny** - commonly called **S[t.] Mary's Church (Kościół Mariacki)** was built in several stages betwee[n] 1343 and 1502. The nave and the tw[o] aisles, the transept and th[e] presbytery have three types of mag[-] nificent vaulting. It is the larges[t] brick church in the world with [a] length of 105.5 m, a width of 48 an[d] 66 m, 28-30 m columns, and an are[a] of ca. 4,900 m². The fifteenth to nine[-] teenth century interior, although in[-] complete, is priceless. The building[s] was rebuilt between 1948-1952, i[n] 1965 it was elevated to the status o[f] Lesser Basilica, and since 1987 it ha[s] been the seat of the Gdańsk Diocese[.] From the top of the tower (76.6 m[)] there is a fantastic view of the cit[y] and its surrounding area. Th[e] church's silhouette has become [a] symbol of the city.

(On the right side) *The partially preserved 46 chord* **organ** *in the organ-loft at the western end of St. Mary's Church was made by the master organ builder Marcin Friese between 1625-1629. It is from St. John's Church (Kościół św. Jana) in Gdańsk. Reconstruction of the instrument from 1980-1985 was inspired by Otton Kulcke, a German Gdańsk citizen, and carried out by the Harry and Guntram Hillebrandt company from Iserhagen, near Hanover. The original Baroque-Mannerist prospect was carved in wood by Peter Brinckmann and Andreas Fischer and polychromed by David van den Block.*

The **main altar** in the presbytery of St. Mary's Church is a late-Gothic polyptych by Master Mich of Augsburg in 1511-1517. The altarpiece (4.89 × 3.90 m) is adorned with monumental figures God the Father, Mary and Christ seated on a tripartite throne under a canopy. The gold-plate and polychromed group majestically depicts the Coronation of the Virgin. The altarpiece is cur rently mounted on a rectangular nineteenth century predella decorated with scenes of the Entom ment. The moveable wings, filled with either sculpted or painted scenes from the life of Chris have been largely reconstructed.

The famous **astronomical clock** located on the northern wall of the northern transept sacrist in St. Mary's Church was made by Hans Düringer between 1464-1470, and it is the tallest of i kind in the world (14 m). This clock was in operation until 1553. Between 1983-1993 it wa reconstructed (70% of elements are original), and now it shows not only the time but the da month and year, the lunar phase, and the positions of the sun and moon in relation to th Zodiac. At noon, scenes of the Annunciation and the Adoration of the Magi appear, the twelv apostles and four evangelists with music playing can be seen in the upper gallery, and Adar and Eve ring bells above them.

The **Royal Chapel (Kaplica Królewska)** is the only Baroque sacral building in the historical heart of Gdańsk. Its patrons were King Jan Sobieski III and Primate Andrzej Olszowski, and it was built in 1678-1681 by Bartłomiej Ranisch in cooperation with the sculptor Andrzej Schlüter the Younger (Młodszy), based on a design by Tylman of Gameren. The chapel is the only example of Counter Reformation architecture in Gdańsk.

Ulica Piwna, fo
merly called Jope
ska, owed its nam
to the beer bran
Jopejskie, brewe
here. Today beer
no longer brewe
here, there are f
wer front stoop
and less of th
Gdańsk "feeling".

The massive, slightly heavy tower of **St. Mary's Church** dominates the city from afar and the street vistas. One of the many legends about the church tower has it that the inhabitants of Gdańsk purposefully did not finish the construction with a pointed cupola to enable a giant called Stolem, who sometimes paid an amicable visit to Gdańsk, to sit on it. The figures on top of the houses are supposed to be his toys that he presented to the friendly burghers.

The **Armoury** or **Arsenal** was constructed as a closing of the vista of Piwna Street. Thus *Antoni van Obberghen* built its facade to resemble the houses' facades. However, the numerous decorative elements such as soldier figures, weapons, exploding grenades and the figure of Athens, the goddess of victory, are an obvious allusion to the building's purpose.

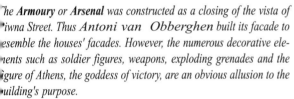

The Salmon Restaurant, which has enjoyed popularity for many centuries (formerly a liquor testing and manufacturing plant), is a symbol of Gdańsk today. The company tradition goes back to 1567 when the Mennonites fled from persecution in the Netherlands and settled down in the vicinity of Gdańsk, in the territory of Żuławy Gdańskie and subsequently further towards Grudziądz. A large group of them settled down in a suburb of Gdańsk called Stare Szkoty. Among them was Kwiryn Vermeulen, an editor of the Bible, whose son, Ambroży is considered the protoplast and founder of the company Der Lachs (Salmon). This sign stuck to the company quite by accident. Thus, after numerous ups and downs and removals, by the time of his successor the company, which manufactured liquors, had found its permanent seat in the Salmon House, which belonged to the Cistercian Monastery. The salmon emblem was merely a guide for those who could not read numbers.

The company continued to be based in this house until 1937, despite the owner changing by inheritance. The company owners, no matter what their surnames were, had always been tradition-minded and unwavering local patriots. Many of them had rendered quite a service to the city. After the trees in the Great Alley were cut down (1813) by the Prussian army, it was owing to funds from the Salmon's owner, Karl Gottfried Henrichsdorf, that the Alley was reconstructed and the trees have survived until today. The company's interiors have, in time, become a museum in its own right as they not only contain a large collection of documents gathered through the centuries, but also a number of Gdańsk craftworks and furniture collected by the owners out of love for the city. The Salmon company made not only Goldwasser, but also other famous liquors such as orange vodka, cherry liqueur known as Karmbambuli, electoral vodka, cumin vodka, rosolis and many, many more. All these liquors were made according to precise recipes which were a business secret (and still are), passed on from one generation to another. Many of the liqueurs and cordials had therapeutic properties for it should be borne in mind that one of the first company owners was a "natural medic" who used cordials as a cure. Songs were sung about these liquors, poems were composed, suffice to mention C.F. Wedekind, G.E. Lessing, H. Von Kleist and E. Hauptman. The best-known verses were written by Adam Mickiewicz in Pan Tadeusz - "this vodka is from Gdańsk, a beverage dear to every Pole; 'Viva! Exclaimed the Judge raising the cask, the city of Gdańsk, once ours, will be ours again! And he poured the silvery liquor around until it started to drop and glitter in the sun.

The apartment house in Szeroka Street completely vanished in the ravages of war, together with its contents. In 1976, in the reconstructed house, the Salmon Restaurant was opened and managed by the Robakowski family from the start. The owners, aware of its immense tradition and prominent position, are doing their best to restore not only the former appearance and atmosphere to the place, but they are also following the principle of continuity of history, of responsibility for the trademark and love for the city. In addition, they are adding new tradition to the old one, as can be seen in the guest book. The restaurant has been visited by such personages as Pope John Paul II, Queen Margaret II of Denmark, Queen Beatrix of the Netherlands, King Harald V of Norway, President of the Czech Republic, President of the Latvian Republic, President of the Republic of Finland, President of the Turkish Republic, George Bush President of the USA, Secretary General of N.A.T.O., Gunter Grass (writer), Charles Aznavour, Margaret Thatcher, G. Schröder, Richard von Weizsäcker, J. Rau.

Such guests are nothing extraordinary for a company whose liquor products have been served at the most exquisite tables at royal courts all over the world for ages!

The damage of 1945 inflicted upon the Gothic hall **church of St. John (Kościół św. Jana)**, dating from the fourteenth and fifteenth centuries, is still being repaired today. A late-Renaissance stone altar from 1599-1612 by Abraham van den Block stands in the church, and the presbytery wall is strongly inclined vertically. The church is currently a concert hall. A charming little lane, one of the characteristic elements of sacral architecture in Gdańsk, encircles the church. This example is the only such fragment that was reconstructed after the destruction of WWII.

(On the next page, above) The **southern facade** of the Gothic hall **church of St. Nicholas (Kościół św. Mikołaja** – a Lesser Basilica since 1928). It was built between 1348-1390, and expanded in the fifteenth century (tower, sacristy, gables, vaulting). Remnants of the church from 1227-1235, which was most probably built in the place of an even earlier temple from the late twelfth century which had been given to the Dominicans by Prince Świętopełek, can be seen in the sacristy basement. On 11 October 1587 King Zygmunt Waza III received the election act. The rich, Gothic (fifteenth century), Renaissance (sixteenth century), and primarily Baroque and Rococo (seventeenth – eighteenth centuries) interior is original as this church was the only one to have survived WWII untouched.

(On the next page, below) The fan vaulting system in the nave of the **St. Nichols Basilica (Bazylika św. Mikołaja)** was executed in the early fifteenth century, the chandelier was made in 1617 by Gerd Benningk, the Rococo pews date to ca. 1780, the late-Baroque pulpit dates from 1715 and the seventeenth and eighteenth century altars near the columns are Baroque and Rococo. In the rear of the presbytery there is a colourful arcade with a Gothic crucifix (1520) by Master Paweł situated on the beam. Other elements here include the monumental late-Renaissance main altar from the 1740's which is richly carved and gold-plated, with the painting of the Apotheosis of St. Nicholas (Apoteoza św. Mikołaja) by August Ranisch (1643) and the late-Gothic choir stalls from the second half of the fifteenth century with their fabulous backs, on which scenes from the life of Christ are depicted.

The metal sculpture of the **Monument to the Defenders of the Polish Post Office (Pomnik Obrońców Poczty Polskiej)** was designed by Wacław Kućma and Krystyna Heyde-Kućma in 1979 and stands on the square in front of the post office to commemorate the heroic 14-hour defense of the Polish post office on 1 September 1939. The building still houses the post office, and also the Museum of Post and Telecommunications (Muzeum Poczty i Telekomunikacji). In the courtyard, there is an interesting bronze bas-relief designed by Zygfryd Korpalski depicting the tragedy of the heroic postal clerks.

Looking down from St. Catherine's - the oldest parish church of Gdańsk - towards the Main Town, we can admire one of the most beautiful views - an abundance of history. The Jacek Tower (formerly "Look into the Kitchen"), the historical market hall, St. Nicolas's Church and the Dominican Monastery, St. Mary's Church in the distance with the apartment houses gathered around like a flock of sheep around a shepherd.

The Jan Sobieski III Monument, dating from 1897 and designed by Tadeusz Barącz, stands at the Wood Market (Targ Drzew-ny). It had originally stood at Wały Het-mańskie in Lvov, it was moved after 1945 to Wilanów Park, and finally to Gdańsk in 1966. To the east a commemorative plaque on a large granite stone tells us that the square is named after Dariusz Kobzdej, the co-founder, in 1979, of the opposition movement known as Ruch Młodej Polski.

The Renaissance **Old Tow Hall (Ratusz Stareg Miasta)** was built by Anto van Obberghen betwee 1587-1595 and is regarde as one of the most fabulo examples of Gdańsk archite ture. The brewer Ja Heweliusz (1611-1687), wh later became a famous a tronomer and was visited b the Polish kings Ja Kazimierz and Ja Sobieski III and other impo tant people, was also a ci councillor and had his offi in this building, not far fro his home on ul. Korzenn The beautiful interior original and it houses work of art from other parts Gdańsk (nineteenth an twentieth centuries).

The fully reconstructed seventeenth century **Miller's Guil** **(Dom Cechu Młynarzy)** is located on the so-called Tarcz or island, in the Radunia Canal (Kanał Raduni). Today it is cafe. The upper part of the western peak of the Great M (Wielki Młyn) and the domed tower of St. Catherine's Churc (Kościół św. Kata-rzyny) can both be seen directly behind

In the spot where three houses belonging to the Hevelius fa mily once stood, which were destroyed in 1945, a **monume** to the outstanding astronomer, actually an excellent brewe was erected in the 1970s.

Almost entirely rebuilt by 1962, the **Great Mill (Wielki Młyn)**, a Gothic construction from ca. 1350, was once one of the largest flour mills in Europe and run on water flowing from the specially built Radunia Canal (ca. 1310) through a system of 18 water wheels. It also boasted its own bakery. Today, it is a shopping centre, but there is an exhibition in the centre which explains how the mill used to work, and a documentary film about the Gdańsk mills can also be viewed.

St. Catherine's Church (Kościół św. Katarzyny), with its three aisles and its separated three-aisle presbytery, is probably the oldest sacred building in Gdańsk. Old-Slavic graves from the tenth to twelfth centuries are in a special crypt in the presbytery. The church was built in stages in the fourteenth and fifteenth centuries. The massive tower is topped with a reconstructed Renaissance dome, known as the Polish type, by Jakub van den Block from 1634. To the east the partially reconstructed presbytery rooftops from the sixteenth century are visible. Inside, 10 types of vaulting combined to create the fabulous ceilings (partly reconstructed). There are also fourteenth and fifteenth century frescoes, a painting from 1510 depicting the Crucifixion (Krzyżowanie), the late-Gothic altar by St. ??? (św. Erazm) (1515), the Renaissance baptismal font from 1585, the great altar by Szymon Herle (1609-1619) with paintings by Antoni Möller and Izaak van den Block, the Hennin epitaph (after 1626), the painting of Christ Entering Jerusalem (Wjazd Chrystusa do Jerozolimy) by Bartłomiej Milwitz (1654), and others.

*The tradition of the **carillon (karylon)**, the set of 49 bells that hang in the tower of **St. Catherine Church (Kościół św. Katarzyny)**, dates to the sixteenth century. Until 1999, it was under renovation as part of the unity and friendship programme between the Polish and German nations. The tower also houses the Museum of Tower Clocks (Muzeum Zegarów Wieżowych).*

*The epitaph of Jan Heweliusz (**Epitafium Jana Heweliusza**) in the presbytery of St. Catherine Church (Kościół św. Katarzy-ny) was made by the Berlin sculptor Meyer in 1779. Its patron was Daniel G. Dawidson, whose maternal great-grandfather had been the famous Gdańsk astronomer. The tombstone, that Heweliusz paid for himself (which used to be in the same location beneath the floor), is next to the pillar with the epitaph. A special case holds a small plaque which was removed from atop the astronomer's coffin.*

St. Bridget's Church (Kościół św. Brygidy) was built in the fourteenth and fifteenth centuries on the site of a former convent, and it was expanded at the beginning of the sixteenth century. It is a hall church with three aisles and a separate presbytery. The tower was built by Bartel Ranisch in 1604 and the dome by Piotr Willer is from 1673. Almost entirely rebuilt between 1971-1975, it has been the shrine of shipyard Solidarność since 1980, and the crosses that have been associated with strikes are displayed here. It has been a Lesser Basilica since 1993. The mostly modern interior was designed by Elżbieta Szczodrowska, Robert Pepliński and Bohdan Pietruszka. Interesting old works of art include the paintings "Allegory of the Triumphant Church" (Alegoria Triumfującego Kościoła) by Herman Han (second half of the sixteenth century) and the colourful "Crucifixion" (Ukrzyżowanie) from the seventeenth century.

The **Monument to the Fallen Shipyard Workers (Pomnik Poległych Stocznio-wców)** was built in 1981 on Solidarność Square in front of Gate no. 2 of the Gdańsk Shipyard to commemorate the heroic shipyard workers and the tragedies they suffered in 1970 and 1980. It is composed of three 48 m tall crosses made of ship steel with three anchors hung from the crosses' transverses (designed by B. Pietruszka). The lower parts of the crosses are decorated with scenes from the lives of the shipyard workers by E. Szczodrowska and R. Pepliński.

The neo-Renaissance **PKP Main Railway Station (Dworzec Główny PKP)** was built after the defensive walls were razed between 1895-1900. The building is dominated by the 48 m water tower with a dome based on the design of the one at the Main Town Hall (Ratusz Głównego Miasta). The renovation of the interior (1995-1997) aroused much controversy, and has become an example of the contempt of the user towards artistically valuable open spaces. Now it seems unchanged but the city is pressing on and the lack of space being devoured by buildings is noticeable.

Corpus Christi Church (**Kościół Bożego Ciała**), built on the site of a hospital outside the old city walls, combines the modesty of the Gothic (main hall 1395-1465) and the Baroque (side aisles 1687-1688, tower 1750-1765). The interior includes a late-Baroque main altar (1768), an organ (1766-1768) made by Friedrich R. Dalitz, a painted ceiling (currently in very poor condition) from 1709 by Carl F. Falckenberg and other elements. A place to commemorate the Gdańsk cemeteries that were destroyed after WWII is planned next to the church.

The middle caponier, blockhouse and the counterscarp gallery that form part of the **Grodzisko Fort** (located behind the PKS bus station) date from 1807-1814 and 1867-1874. This is a good place to contemplate and admire the nineteenth century art of fortification building. Vicious battles for Gdańsk, fought by the Russian, Saxon and Napoleonic armies, took place here in 1734 and 1807. The site was expanded in the seventeenth century, although it had been used as a defensive position as early as the middle ages. A 20 m tall metal cross was placed on the Grodzisko in 2000. There is a great view of Gdańsk from this vantage point.

A utility building adjacent to the New Town Hall. It used to be a coach house and a stable.

St. Elizabeth's Church (Kościół św. Elżbiety – late fourteenth century) is a single aisle Gothic church built on the site of a former hospital. It has an interesting suspended tower above the entrance, and its presbytery was added by August Stüler in 1846. From the second half of the sixteenth century it was Calvinistic, and later (1846) it became a garrison church. Its modest interior includes a stained-glass window made by Zofia Baudouin de Courtenay in 1952.

The **New Town Hall**. The building was erected in the 1800s as the headquarters of the commandment of the Gdańsk garrison. In the period between the two wars the High Commissioner of the Nations League resided here, working as an arbitrator in the conflicts between Poland and the Free City of Gdańsk. From after the war up to the 1980s the building housed the famous Students of the Coast Club "Żak". It is from here that such talents as Zbigniew Cybulski, Bogumił Kobiela, Jacek Fedorowicz and Czesław Niemen set off to make their mark in the wider world. Nowadays it serves as the seat of the Gdańsk City Council. An enormous building on the right is the former Provincial Committee of the former Polish United Workers' Party (PZPR). It was this building that was set on fire, which sparked off the incidents of December 1970.

This place, called **Mały Błędnik**, was created after the levelling of the ramparts and has survived with only slight alterations until today as a green enclave. The houses in the background were destroyed in 1945 and Wały Jagiellońskie Street was built there.

The inhabitants of Gdańsk, striving to continue the tradition of their "city salon", start and finish all major public events in Długa Street and the Long Market, as they did ages ago. One of many such events is **St. Dominic's Fair**, the most important tourist and commercial event of the year.

One of the major open-air events in recent years was the celebration of the millennium of Gdańsk in 1997. The street theatre plays, shows and cultural events impressed the observer with their splendor. The key attraction of St. Dominic's Fair, the flea market - a collectors' exchange - had to give up its precedence at that time.

The Franciscan **Church of the Holy Trinity (Kościół św. Trójc** – 1481-1514) is a Gothic three-aisled hall church with beautif gables, that separate the eastern side reading room, a rarity i Poland, from the earlier presbytery (formerly the Church of th Lord's Supper (Kościół Wieczerzy Pańskiej) from 1422-1431 The Chapel of St. Ann (kaplica św. Anny – 1480-1484), desig nated for Poles, is located on the southern side of the church. T the church's north is the residential Pulpit House (Dor Kazalnicowy) that was built based on skeleton construction. Th main church interior includes nine Gothic stalls (1510-1511), Renaissance pulpit (1541), the epitaph of the Marquis Giovann B. B. d'Oria (1597), the wonderful spider (1653) and other work The chapel interior has an altar, a loft with an organ (1710), pulpit (1721) and an altar painting of the Return of the Prodig Son (Powrót syna marnotrawnego – seventeenth century). T the south is the former monastery building (1481-1514), once part of this large monastic complex, which functioned as a scho (1558), was home to the famous Academic Gymnasiun (Gimnazjum Akademickie – 1580), and later became a museu (1872). Today, it houses the Gdańsk Branch of the Nationa Museum (Muzeum Narodowe). The ground floor houses pe manent exhibits of Gdańsk furniture, altars, sculpture, wood car ers grates, china, garments, liturgical ornaments, etc., an exter sive collection of paintings from the fifteenth to twentieth cent ries is located on the first floor, and the second floor is used fo temporary exhibitions.

The famous Gothic **triptych of the Last Judgement (Sąd Ostateczny)** by the renowned Flemish painter Hans Memling (1472 - 1473) is the most valuable work in the collections of the Gdańsk Branch of the National Museum (on loan from St. Mary's Church). The painting's patrons, the Italian Angelo Tani and his wife Catherine - with ties to the Medici family, are depicted on the exterior of the side wings that are visible when the triptych is closed (following photograph).

*The **Wisłoujście Fortress**, unique in Europe, once protected the Vistula River mouth through which ships sailed into Gdańsk port on the Motława River. The lighthouse tower from 1482 which was later surrounded by walls, towers and moats reminds visitors of the great maritime city Gdańsk once was.*
*The **Bastion of St. Gertrude (Bastion św. Gertrudy)** closes the western end of the defensive fortifications of old Gdańsk (designed by Antoni van Obberghen and built at the end of the sixteenth century) and is patterned after neo-Italianate fortifications. Next to this is the **Bison Bastion (Bastion Żubr** - correctly Aurochs (Tur) that was built in the Dutch*

manner by Corneliusz van der Bosch between 1621-1629. These two structures are surrounded by a wonderful view of the city, the edge of the Gdańsk Heights (Wysoczyzna Gdańska), the residential quarters of Zaroślak, Nowe Szkoty and Orunia, and bastions, moats and the Żuławy Gdańskie area.

The **stone sluice** is an singularly outstanding hydrotechnical project, in European terms. It was designed and built by Willem J. Benning and Adrian Olbrants in 1619-1624. The lock regulates the water level in the Motława River and in the moats. The ruins of a grain water mill stand next to it.

Ships and ferries entering Gdańsk port are welcomed by a tall monument made of stone blocks, standing on an equally high mound (25 m). It commemorates the 2nd World War and all sites at which Polish soldiers lost their lives. Regardless of the past controversies around the monument and the development of the historical area of Westerplatte, this place has become symbolic for generations of Poles and some Europeans.

The sailing ships that visit Gdańsk port during rallies or a major sailing event are merely reminiscent of the atmosphere in the port canal in the old days.

Jaśkowa Dolina *is a charming part of the Gdańsk district of Wrzeszcz. It was once a favorite place for walks, relaxation and outdoor games for the ric of Gdansk, who began building summer residences (palaces) here in the seventeenth century.*

The **Gutenberg Grove (Gaj Gutenberga)** *with a gazebo and statue (reconstructed) is located near Jaśkowa Dolina on a moraine hill. It was built in the late-nineteenth century by the Gdańsk Printers' Guild (Gdański Cech Drukarzy) to commemorate Johannes Gutenberg, the inventor of the printing press. A copy of his original work, the famous Gutenberg Bible from ca. 1455, is kept in the Diocese Museum (Muzeum Diecezjalne) in Pelplin, a small town near Gdańsk.*

Grass's Bench - situated in Wrzeszcz in Józef Wybicki Square. The figure of Oskar with his inseparable drum is a reminder that not far from this place - in 13 Lelewela Street - in 1927, Günter Grass was born, a winner of the Nobel Prize for literature, the author of the well-known Tin Drum and many more boks.

Pacholek hill (100.8 m above sea level), close to Oliwa Cathedral, was most likely once a cult site for Pomeranian pagans, has been known as a vantage poir since the late eighteenth century. From atop the 20 m platform, erected in 1975, there is a beautiful view of Sopot, the Gulf of Gdańsk, Oliwa and other Gdańs quarters, the Gdańsk Heights (Wysoczyzna Gdańska) and the Valley of Joy (Dolina Radości). The layout of the Cistercian abbey in Oliwa, including the churc and monastery to the south, the two abbey palaces, the park and grange, and the parish church of St. James (św Jakuba), is especially clear.

*The famous post-Cistercian **Church of the Hor Trinity, St. Mary and St. Bernard (Kościół śv Trójcy, NMP and św. Bernarda)** has been com monly referred to as Oliwa Cathedral since th inception of the Diocese of Gdańsk here in 192C It has been a Lesser Basilica since 1971. The 10 m long building is three-aisled with a transvers nave, a presbytery and an ambulatory. Traces c different architectural styles, from the Roman esque oratory (ca. 1200) to twentieth century e ements, can be seen throughout the church. It rich decoration also originates from various pe riods from the fifteenth to the twentieth centuries*

The Rococo **main organ** in Oliwa Cathedral (Katedra Oliwska) with its 110 chords and 7,876 organ-pipes, is the outstanding work of the Cistercian monk Michał (Jan Wulf of Orneta) dating from 1763-1788. It was completed by the master organist Friedrich R. Dalitz in 1791-1793. Its fantastic semi-elliptical prospect, a rarity in Europe, with statues of angels, movable trumpets and trombones, suns and stars was made in a local workshop under the supervision of the brothers Alanus and Józef Gross.

The Baroque **main altar** in the presbytery of Oliwa Cathedral is from 1688 and its patron was Abbot Michał A. Hacki. The 7 m tall colonnade is its main feature, in the middle of which is an Andreas Stech painting "The Adoration of Mary with Admirers" (Adoracja Marii z adorantami). Above the colonnade's entablature is a concave space made of stucco and decorated with a starry sky, approximately 150 angel's heads, and characters from both the Old and New Testaments.

A late-Baroque **pulpit** in Oliwa Cathedral, from the second half of the eighteenth century, is located to the left of the presbytery. It was made in a local workshop, its walls are decorated with panels featuring scenes from the life and works of St. Bernard, and the acoustic canopy is decorated with figures.

The patron of the **tomb of the Pomeranian Princes (grobowiec książąt pomorskich)** of 1615 was Abbot Dawid Konarski. Made of black marble and featuring an image of a griffin, it stands in the northern transept of Oliwa Cathedral and once covered the entrance to the crypt in the presbytery where the ashes of east-Pomeranian Princes and their family members still rest.

The late-Renaissance **altar of the Holy Trinity (ołtarz św. Trójcy)** on the eastern wall of the northern wing of the transverse nave in Oliwa Cathedral is a marvelous example of the local Cistercian workshop which was well-known in Poland for many years. Its patron was Rafał Kos, a Cistercian monk from Oliwa. The altar, from 1606, has three levels and is richly decorated with sculptures, paintings and especially polychromes made by Wolfgang Sporer (Spor).

*The new **Abbots' Palace (Pałac Opatów)**, behind the lawns and flower-beds in the French park of Oliwa Park is surrounded by four trimmed yews from the second half of the eighteenth century. The palace was built in the seventeenth century, later to be expanded by Abbot Józef J. Rybiński in 1754-1756. It was rebuilt after being destroyed by fire in 1945, and it has been home to a museum since 1926.*

The alley, formed by specially shaped trees whose branches and leaves create a roof, is in the northern part of Oliwa Park (Park Oliwski), is adjacent to the eastern pond which is an extension of the famous Linden-tree Lane (Aleja Lipowa). The park's origins date to the sixteenth or seventeenth centuries. The Cistercian Abbot Rybiński ordered the park to be redesigned in 1760, and the new park was built in the French style by Kazimierz Dębiński from Kock, who had designed the Wilanów Park. By 1792, the park had been expanded on its northern side, and the new area was laid out in the English style by Johannes G. Salzmann.

Oliwa once used to bustle with life and work. On the tiny Oliwa Stream, Cistercian monks managed to build 14 industrial plants, smithies, sawmills, fullers' mills and gunpowder factories. A large part of this industrial "basin" working to provide for the needs of Gdańsk has survived until now. The best-preserved historical monument is the **water smithy** in the Schwabe Valley, dating back to the 1500s. It had been continuously running until 1948. It used the energy of the water in the seemingly small stream. In the stream, however, there is a big difference of levels and even a slight swelling had a huge capacity for generating energy. It now houses a branch of the Technology Museum.

In the **Krzaczasty Młyn Valley** there once (19th c.) used to be a romantic lodging house, founded by a miller, which was so frequently visited due to the beauty of the location, that the miller decided to make money on it. Since the 1950s there has been a constantly growing **zoological garden** in this area. The garden is one of the most picturesquely situated in Europe and it has had significant successes in animal breeding. It is worth visiting and walking in its alleys.

SOPOT

Sopot is situated in between Gdańsk and Gdynia - on the edge of the Gdańsk Upland - covered with forests intersected with many valleys and ravines, formed by the Scandinavian glacier - and by the seaside. Thanks to its location, Sopot has a very favourable climate. Its insolation is relatively long, the air humidity is suitable and the daily temperature is rather balanced. The sea and sandy beach are the principal assets of the city. This is the place for sunbathing and swimming.

The first reference to Sopot dates from 1283, when this small fishing village was presented to the Cistercian monks of Oliwa by Pomeranian Prince Mściwoj II. The monks managed Sopot for almost five hundred years. After the 1st partition of Poland in 1772, Sopot fell into German hands.

The excellent location and climatic features of Sopot had been discovered earlier. From the mid-1500s wealthy patricians of Gdańsk and foreign diplomats started to build their impressive summer mansions in Sopot. This is when the first attempts at organising special places for bathing in the sea were made. But the bathing centre flourished some time later. After Napoleon's defeat in Russia and the withdrawal of the French army from Moscow, a surgeon and major, J.J. Haffner settled in Gdańsk. He bought a plot of land in Sopot and built a bathing house (baths) in 1823. The following year he erected the Spring House and then established the nearby park, still in existence. He also laid out walking paths and constructed the first pier. Obviously, the first visitors wishing to restore their stamina and health started coming to Sopot. The city was recognised as a seaside resort. Following the opening of a railway connection between Koszalin, Gdańsk and Warsaw in 1870, Sopot started to develop rapidly. A new Spring House was built and in 1901 Sopot was granted municipal rights. The still existing Balneological Centre was built in 1903. Among the treatments it offered were various baths including sea water baths, radiation, massages, and mud baths. Poles were amongst the most frequent visitors to the spa.

Sopot gradually become a very fashionable spot in Europe - it was known as the "Riviera of the North". The city became more and more beautiful, it acquired tennis courts, a hippodrome, new houses and many stately villas. Finally, in 1909, the famous **Forest Opera** was opened. Before the 1st World War, Sopot was a renowned and famous European seaside resort with direct sea connections to Europe. After the Treaty of Versailles, Sopot became part of the Free City of Gdańsk.

In 1920 a casino was founded and in 1927 the charming and majestic **Grand Hotel** was opened. The wooden pier was extended to its present length of 516 metres. While strolling along Sopot pier one could come across celebrities, diplomats, artists and aristocrats. The Pearl of the Baltic was flourishing.

After 1945 Sopot continued to be fashionable. It attracts a huge number of men of letters and artists: poets, writers, painters, musicians, composers and actors. Many of them settle down in Sopot. Its ambiance is favourable for artists. The ambiance can be felt by everybody. Sopot has a unique atmosphere and style which can be sensed everywhere. Sopot, today inhabited by some 50 thousand people, is the venue of many artistic and sports events at a European level. The high street of Sopot - **Bohaterów Monte Cassino**, nicknamed "Monciak" - plays the role of the city's central promenade. Each visitor to Sopot has to show off here in his/her latest outfit - even the most avante-guardist or eccentric clothing comes as no surprise. Its numerous cafés, tiny shops, galleries and cultural events entice tourists and the colourful crowd "floating" towards the pier gives the impression of a never-ending party at the right place and in good company. A party going on until the small hours.

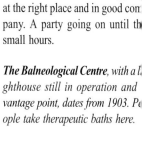

The Balneological Centre, with a lighthouse still in operation and a vantage point, dates from 1903. People take therapeutic baths here.

The **fountain** located opposite the base of the pier is an important historic monument. Built before the First World War, it impressed the public with its colourful illumination and its great height of over 20 m. The area surrounding it, including the Spa-house, medicinal baths, concert shell and promenade were modernised in the 1930s, only to be significantly changed after WWII.

Sopot's **Grand Hotel** (formerly the **Casino Hotel**) was built in 1924-1927. This distinctive hotel is located almost directly on the beach, and has hosted many important people, politicians, artists and businessmen, and its most famous room is the General's Apartment (Apartament Generalski) in which General Charles de Gaulle stayed. As in every respected hotel, there is no room 13. A fantastic view of the hotel from the pier is reminiscent of the good old days of Sopot.

St. George's Church in Bohaterów Monte Cassino Street is a parish and garrison church. It was built in the neo-gothic style in 1899-1901, thanks to the generosity of the Caesarian couple. Empress Augusta Victoria and her husband Wilhelm II donated money to build the temple and the Kaiser himself approved the construction design, raising the tower to 40 meters to make it visible to sailors and fishermen at sea. The consecration ceremony of the brick-and-stone building was attended by the Empress on 17 September 1901. Inside the church, one cannot miss the relief of God's Mother with Child, originally on board the passenger ship "Batory".

In the square in front of the church there is a little chapel from 1909 with the figure of St. Wojciech and one of the oldest existing coats of arms of Sopot.

Today, **Bohaterów Monte Cassino Street**, commonly known as Monciak, is not only a fashionable promenade. Until the 1800s it was one of the main communication routes in the fishing village of Sopot. It also connected the farm, situated higher up (in the vicinity of Al. Niepodległości), and several summerhouses of wealthy inhabitants of Gdańsk with the seashore that was frequented as willingly as today, even for therapeutic purposes. Among the bathers was also Hetman Jan Sobieski with his wife, Marysieńka (on the beach in the nearby Kolibki).

Every visitor to Sopot is obliged to show up in this street. In summer it is difficult to walk here - a colourful crowd of tourists, spa visitors and inhabitants floods the street all day long and almost all night. The historical buildings in Monciak come from the 19th and 20th centuries, but modern times have also left their "traces". The street fragment shown in the photo with the shopping centre Monte embedded in the old architecture and the McDonalds not far away are an excellent illustration of a functional marriage of the past with the present. The glass wall of Monte reflects the tower of St. George's.

In summer **Monte Cassino Street** fills up with many open-air cafes where you can sit down and look around, drink a nice cup of coffee and chat with friends, maybe spot a celebrity. The theatre, cinema, artist cafes and pubs, galleries and little corner shops with a long tradition make up the ambiance of the street. Artists exhibit their works and various buskers (the photo shows a Ukrainian "did") by playing their music, add colour to the high street of the health resort of Sopot.

The **Spa Square** (Plac Zdrojowy) ends the famous Monciak of Sopot running towards the sea. A **fountain with a fisherman's** figure, installed here in 1998, reminds us of the fishing roots of the town. A perfect resting place on hot days.

The **Forest Opera (Opera Leśna)** is today the unquestionable symbol of Sopot, and a monument to Polish song, although the current theatre is nothing like the original. The small forest valley with great natural acoustics was discovered in the late nineteenth century. During the summer season spa visitors eagerly walked up here to listen to special solo concerts. The first professional concert theatre was built in 1909 and renowned Wagner festivals took place here. The theatre has been modernised many times since WWII, especially to facilitate TV transmissions. The light-weight canopy which stretches over the audience of five thousand was added in 1961. Today, the theatre is fully modernised, and the primary advantages of the site, its natural acoustics, are neither known nor even important. The International Song Festival, known in Europe and beyond, has been held in the Forest Opera since 1965.

The **Sopot Fishermen's Chapel** was financed with the collections of the inhabitants of Sopot to commemorate the visit of Pope John Paul II to Sopot in June 1999. Since the 13th c. Sopot has had a **Fishing Port** where you can buy fresh fish straight from the cutter, or smoked fish. The drying nets and boats on the beach are a reminder of the slowly vanishing fisherman's profession, so romantic, yet dangerous.

GDYNIA

Gdynia is the third constituent of the Tri-City and its modern character ideally complements and adds colour to the other two: the historical, one-thousand-year-old Gdańsk and the health resort of Sopot.

Gdynia symbolises the development of Polish maritime industry as the fulfillment of the dreams of many enlightened Poles, who regarded it as the foundation of the country's independence and freedom.

Gdynia was first mentioned in a document, dated 1253, as a village belonging to a parish in Oksywie. At first it was the property of the Cistercian Order from Oliwa, then of Jan of Różęcin, who in 1382 presented this farming and fishing village to the Carthusian Order he had brought to Kartuzy. Gdynia belonged to the Carthusians for nearly 400 years, until the 1st partition of Poland (1772). During that time it was burnt twice and reconstructed; afterwards it fell under the Prussian rule for about 150 years - until the end of the 1st World War.

At the beginning of the 20th century, owing to its convenient location by the sea, Gdynia started to evolve into a seaside holiday resort, more and more often visited by Poles from the interior.

In 1920, when the independent Republic of Poland regained access to the sea, a new period in Gdynia's history commenced. It was then that the decision was taken to construct a naval port in Gdynia. The main designer of the port was engineer Tadeusz Wenda, at the head of a team of excellent professionals. The regaining of independence and access to the sea by Poland stirred up incredible enthusiasm in people, which gave the port construction an equally astonishing momentum. By April 1923 a temporary port was open and in August the first seagoing ship, the S.S. Kentucky, sailed to Gdynia under the French flag. As a result of the next steps of the construction work, the commercial, fishing and passenger port came into being (in 1930 the first regular passenger line Gdynia-New York was launched). By 1934 Gdynia had become the leading Baltic port with respect to the volume of goods/freight handled and the most modern one in Europe.

Together with the port a new city was emerging. According to the first post-war census, in 1921 there were 1,268 inhabitants in Gdynia. In 1926, the year of granting municipal rights, Gdynia already had 12,000 inhabitants and in 1939 this had multiplied to 127,000! In a decade a small fishing village turned into a modern town with modern infrastructure, active cultural and scientific life, the indisputable pride of inter-war Poland.

The 2nd World War caused significant damage to the port and part of the city. The reconstruction of Gdynia and its development up to the present day clearly prove that the Gdynia phenomenon lives on. The dynamic development of the port (the container terminal), the shipyard and the city placed, and continues to place, Gdynia in the first position among the fastest developing Polish cities. This 250-thousand people city has left its mark in the latest history of Poland. In December 1970 shipyard workers and inhabitants of Gdynia protested against the established political order. People were killed and wounded, and today these tragic events are commemorated by the monument to the Victims of December'70 near the Gdynia Shipyard and the 23-metre-tall cross near the City Hall.

Gdynia also offers numerous tourist attractions: Oksywie, with the picturesquely situated church and one of the most beautiful Polish cemeteries overlooking the sea, the famous Kościuszko Square - the city tourist centre, the destroyer museum "Błyskawica", the sailing ships "Dar Pomorza" and "Dar Młodzieży", the Sea Aquarium and the Oceanographic Museum, the marina, the Music Theatre with its international repertoire, the sandy beach, the Navy Museum, Świętojańska Street, Kamienna Góra Hill, sailing ships, boats, water sports and the romantic district of Orłowo with its wooden pier, beach, seaside summer theatre and nature reserve.

Gdynia stands for continuous progress: it is a very ambitious and modern city, unafraid of challenges, whose imaginative, sea-loving inhabitants fearlessly look to the future.

*The **tall-ship** Dar Pomorza is moored at the Pomeranian Quay of the South Pier (Nabrzeże Pomorskie Mola Południowego) and is today a museum. Previously, it was a training ship for the Maritime Academy, and it sailed around the world many times carrying students and future officers of the merchant*

fleet. The ship played an important educational role for the crews of the Polish fleet, and when it was retired, due to age and its technical state, it was replaced with the very similar modern sailing ship, "Dar Młodzieży". As a matter of fact, youths from all over Poland contributed financially to the building of the ship which the Gdynia Maritime Academy owns.

From the vantage point at **Stone Hill (Kamienna Góra)** (52.4 m above sea level) one can see the General M. Zaruski yacht harbour, the outer part of the port and the South Pier, the breakwater, the roadstead in the Gulf of Gdańsk, the Hel Peninsula in good weather, and the housing estates of Gdynia. The once small Kashubian village has been a dynamically developing city since 1920.

The **Gdynia marina** can hold up to 120 yachts (at a time), sailing in to the city from all over the world.

The **destroyer ORP "Błyskawica"** was built in England in 1937. It actively participated in the 2nd WW. Since 1976 it has served as a museum ship illustrating the history and tradition of the Polish Navy.

In 1988, near the seaside boulevard a monument To Those who Left for an Eternal Watch was unveiled, to commemorate the fishermen and sailors lost at se (on the next page, top).

At the end of the Southern Pier there are two monuments: a metal one, "A Game of Masts" and a stone one, to the memory of one of the best maritime writers Joseph Conrad Korzeniowski (on the next page, bottom).

Kościuszko Square (Skwer Kościuszki) and the South Pier (Molo Południowe) form a beautiful open area, and it is not a coincidence that several importan Gdynia monuments are located here. The fountain, built in the 1970s, is special with its sea-green water and its original illumination.

Ulica Świętojańska is the most important street in Gdynia and nearly a promenade. To the left is the Church of the Blessed Virgin Mary (Kościół Najświętszej Marii Panny). During the years of communist stagnation, the small shops that were located here, supplied with western goods by returning sailors, was a window on the world for the entire Tri-City.

CHIPOLBROK. The seat of the Chinese-Polish Joint-Stock Shipping Company and the Austrian consulate in the impressive building at 17 Śląska Street are examples of the modern architecture of the present-day Gdynia.

(On the right side) The main office of PROKOM at 23-25 Śląska Street is another example of the modern architecture of Gdynia and evidence that major companies, banks and institutions choose to establish themselves in the city.

The **"Batory" Department Store** at the crossroads of 10 Lutego and Władysława IV Streets was opened in 1998. The building is shaped like a ship with two prominent chimneys and the name Batory refers to the recent history of the Polish passenger fleet and its transatlantic liners, whose most prominent representative was MV "Batory", which sailed under the Polish flag for 33 years.

The **first pier** (175 m - partially reconstructed) **in Orłowo**, currently a district of Gdynia, was built in 1934 as a landing for the Vistula Ship Company that sailed between Tczew and Gdynia. The tall cliff that rises above the shore is a part of the Redłowo Hillock (Kępa Redłowska - 90.8 m above sea level), a protected nature reserve which includes the shoreline.

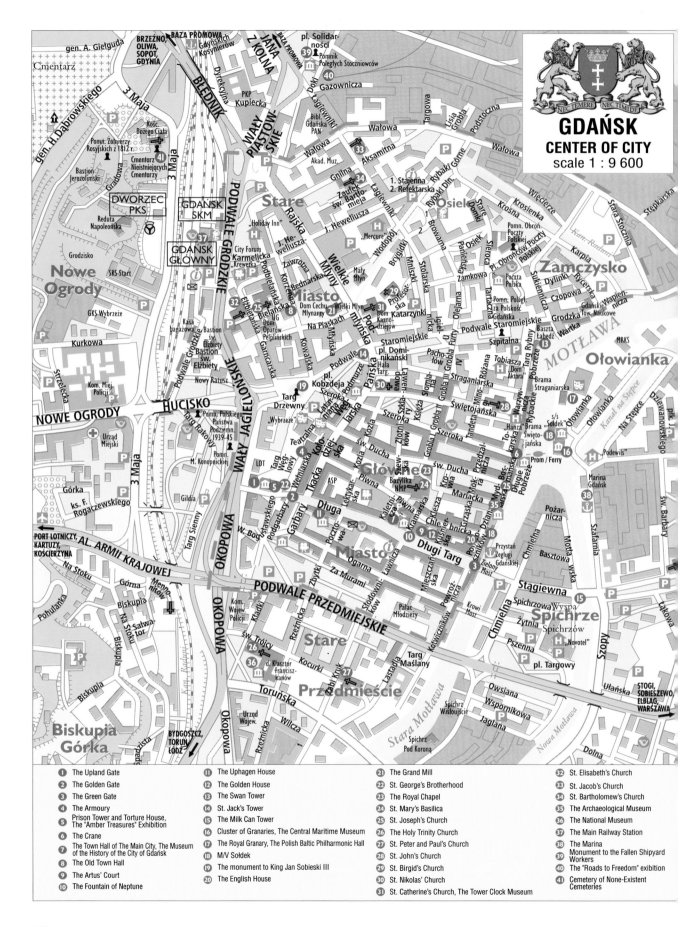

❶	The Upland Gate	⓫	The Uphagen House	㉑	The Grand Mill	㉜	St. Elisabeth's Church
❷	The Golden Gate	⓬	The Golden House	㉒	St. George's Brotherhood	㉝	St. Jacob's Church
❸	The Green Gate	⓭	The Swan Tower	㉓	The Royal Chapel	㉞	St. Bartholomew's Church
❹	The Armoury	⓮	St. Jack's Tower	㉔	St. Mary's Basilica	㉟	The Archaeological Museum
❺	Prison Tower and Torture House, The "Amber Treasures" Exhibition	⓯	The Milk Can Tower	㉕	St. Joseph's Church	㊱	The National Museum
❻	The Crane	⓰	Cluster of Granaries, The Central Maritime Museum	㉖	The Holy Trinity Church	㊲	The Main Railway Station
❼	The Town Hall of The Main City, The Museum of the History of the City of Gdańsk	⓱	The Royal Granary, The Polish Baltic Philharmonic Hall	㉗	St. Peter and Paul's Church	㊳	The Marina
❽	The Old Town Hall	⓲	M/V Sołdek	㉘	St. John's Church	㊴	Monument to the Fallen Shipyard Workers
❾	The Artus' Court	⓳	The monument to King Jan Sobieski III	㉙	St. Birgid's Church	㊵	The "Roads to Freedom" exibition
❿	The Fountain of Neptune	⓴	The English House	㉚	St. Nikolas' Church	㊶	Cemetery of None-Existent Cemeteries
				㉛	St. Catherine's Church, The Tower Clock Museum		

128